The Atonement

and Other Writings

The
Atonement

and Other Writings

by Zane C. Hodges

Introduction by Shawn C. Lazar

The Atonement and Other Writings
Copyright © 2014 by Grace Evangelical Society
4851 S I-35 E, Suite 203
Corinth, TX 76210
www.faithalone.org
ges@faithalone.org
940-270-8827

Hodges, Zane C., 1932-2008

ISBN 978-0-9883472-3-6

Edited by Shawn C. Lazar

Printed in the United States of America

*To Luis Rodriguez, Tony Evans,
and Dick & Anne Caddock,
dear friends in Christ.*

Table of Contents

Introduction

Zane C. Hodges (1932-2008) devoted his life and ministry to expounding God's Word. He taught New Testament Greek and Exegesis at Dallas Theological Seminary for 27 years, while preaching at Victor Street Bible Chapel, a Hispanic assembly in East Dallas, for 50 years. Continuing in the Plymouth Brethren tradition of radical Biblical exegesis, Hodges's conclusions often brought him into conflict with long-standing theological traditions, but his devotion to the Word made him a fearless defender of its truths, whether these were popular or not.

This volume collects three of Hodges's longer essays, formerly printed as booklets, which have been long out of print and hard to find. They are titled *The Atonement, Did Paul Preach Eternal Life? Should We?*, and *Jesus, God's Prophet*. Each booklet is a theological goldmine.

Theories of the Atonement

In the first section, Hodges addresses the nature and extent of the atonement. Most Evangelicals think of the atonement as a package deal. Calvinists thinks the benefits of the atonement are only available to the elect and will be applied at the moment God sovereignly chooses to regenerate the person. Arminians take the view that the benefits of the cross are potentially available to all, but are only applied to believers at the moment of faith (or for sacramental traditions, at baptism). If someone does not believe (or is not baptized), their sins remain unforgiven, and they will be sent to hell as a punishment for them.

But Hodges took a different view. In *The Atonement*,[1] Hodges denies the Bible speaks of the benefits of the atonement as an all or nothing affair. Some benefits are automatically available to all, while others are only potentially available to believers. Some of the universal benefits include Jesus being the propitiation for the whole world (1 John 2:2), becoming sin for everyone (2 Cor 5:21), and actually taking away the sin of the world (John 1:29).

However, recognizing these universal effects does not lead Hodges to a doctrine of universalism (the idea that everyone will be eternally saved). He affirms that people still go to hell, but not as a punishment for their sins. How so? Hodges shows there is an important difference between not having our sins imputed to us, and being given eternal life. God has reconciled the world to Himself, but He hasn't given everlasting life to everyone. That gift is reserved for believers alone. Anyone who does not believe in Jesus for eternal life will go to hell, not as God's punishment for their sins, but because hell is the self-inflicted natural consequence of lacking God's own eternal life.

Needless to say, readers will find that Hodges challenges many of their most cherished theological assumptions about what happened on the cross.

The Language of Eternal Life

In the second section, Hodges examines the doctrine of eternal life. Ever since Luther first re-discovered the Pauline language of justification by faith alone, it has become the *sine qua non* of Protestant evangelism. But many in the Free Grace movement have come to prefer the Johannine language of *eternal life* as a simpler and more comprehensive way to describe the full spectrum of God's gift of eternal salvation. In *Did Paul Preach Eternal Life?*, Hodges shows that even though Paul is known for his doctrine of justification, he also preached the message of eternal life throughout his ministry. Neglecting this aspect of Paul's ministry, or emphasizing

---

[1] We have also included two articles that Hodges wrote, which further explain his view of the atonement: "What Do We Mean by Propitiation?" and "The Sin of Unbelief," which appear as chapters 5 and 6 respectively.

justification to the exclusion of eternal life, means neglecting an essential part of Pauline theology.

God's Prophet

Finally, in the third section, Hodges turns to the subject of eschatology. In *Jesus, God's Prophet*, Hodges examines the Olivet Discourse, showing how Jesus brought fresh revelation about the end times. As Hodges takes us through the prophecies, we learn about a coming worldwide disaster, the difference between prepared and unprepared servants, the necessity of abiding in Jesus, rewards and the possibility of eternal loss, and the fate of those living at the time of the Second Coming, among other topics. In short, *Jesus, God's Prophet* is an enlightening summary of Biblical eschatology, as preached by Jesus Himself.

Conclusion

Despite their relative brevity, each of these booklets represent a wealth of spiritual teaching, condensed by Hodges from a lifetime of studying and preaching the Bible. Readers will find in them a provocative and invaluable resource for understanding Biblical soteriology and eschatology.

Shawn Lazar
Corinth, TX
February 16, 2014

Part 1
The Atonement

CHAPTER 1

If Christ Died for All, Why Aren't We All Saved?

It is always appropriate to think carefully about the atoning work of our Lord and Savior Jesus Christ. As most Christians know, the Son of God came into the world to offer himself on the cross as a sacrifice for the sins of all humanity. John the Baptist proclaimed Him as "the Lamb of God who takes away the sin of the world" (John 1:29).

Some forms of theology, however, find this a difficult proposition to accept without reservation. They often state that if Christ indeed died for all, then all will in fact be saved. But, since the Bible teaches that many are not going to be saved, they conclude that Christ could not have died for the sins of the lost. This leads to a doctrine called "limited atonement," which is the claim that Christ really only died for the elect (that is, for those God had chosen to be saved).

But even those who reject a doctrine of limited atonement sometimes have problems with the idea that Christ paid for the sins of all human beings. Thus they are inclined to qualify the atonement by saying that Christ *potentially* paid for the sins of every person. For those who put it this way, if unsaved people do not accept the work of the cross, then they will pay for their own sins in hell forever.

Neither of the two ideas that we have just mentioned is acceptable in the light of Scripture. The Bible is quite straightforward in declaring that Christ died for everybody. Not only is this stated plainly in 2 Cor 5:19, but also in 1 John 2:2, where we read, "And He Himself is the propitiation for our sins, and not for ours only but also for the whole world."

15

In both of these passages the *world* is the object of Christ's reconciling work on the cross. There is not the slightest hint that this
is not really quite true, but only true *potentially*. In fact, 2 Cor 5:19
tells us that in the work of the cross God was "*not imputing* their
trespasses to them" (emphasis added). There is no room in this
straightforward statement for the idea of potentiality. The same is
equally true of 1 John 2:2.

At the same time, the idea that the word "world" in these passages refers to "the world of the elect" is farfetched. Although this
explanation is often claimed by five-point Calvinists, it is an obvious example of special pleading. No such usage of the term "world"
is to be found anywhere in the New Testament.

Both 2 Cor 5:19 and 1 John 2:2 must be taken at face value. The
Lord Jesus paid for everyone's sins. Thus the work of the cross is
splendid and staggering in its universal scope: No human being has
ever lived for whom Christ did not effectively die! So why doesn't
God save everybody?

One answer to this question is actually found in 2 Cor 5:21. In
this famous concluding verse of that chapter, we are told: "For He
[God] made Him [Christ] who knew no sin to be sin for us, that we
might become the righteousness of God in Him." In other words,
the Lord Jesus Christ bore all our sins in order that we, the sinners, might acquire the very righteousness of God in Christ. That
this truth is also one of the great themes of the book of Romans
will probably be evident to most readers of this chapter (see Rom
3:21-22).

But also quite clear in 2 Cor 5:21 is the fact that Christ's death
does not *automatically* confer God's righteousness. Instead, as Paul
emphasizes in Romans, that righteousness is acquired by faith. So
Paul states in 2 Cor 5:21 that the Lord Jesus was "made...to be sin
for us, *that* [Greek: in order that] we might" (emphasis added) have
God's righteousness.

Eternal salvation is therefore a two step process. The first step has
already been taken: the righteous justice of God was satisfied for all
humanity by the death of Christ. That is, at the cross God was "reconciling the world to Himself" by "not imputing their trespasses
to them" (2 Cor 5:19). But the second step is for sinners themselves
to be "reconciled to God" (2 Cor 5:20). This happens, of course,

when they believe in Christ and, in consequence of that, become "the righteousness of God in Him" (2 Cor 5:21).

Another way of saying the same thing is this; the death of Christ changes the world's relationship to God, its Judge. It does this because, on the cross, Jesus bore the penalty of God's holy justice for everyone. However, the sinner's individual relationship to God is still one of complete estrangement that can only be changed by the experience of justification/regeneration by faith.

An illustration may help. Suppose a man is found guilty of a crime, but his sentence is served by an innocent substitute (granted, not a likely occurrence in our day). If the court has accepted the substitute's experience of the penalty, the guilty party will never be sentenced for that crime. But now, suppose that the guilty man has a relationship of enmity with the judge who presides over his case. Will the judge allow this man to live at the judge's house and partake of the same benefits as the rest of the judge's family? Hardly, unless something happens that reconciles the guilty party to the judge.

Revelation 20:11-15 makes clear that each man's "works" are assessed at the final judgment (verifying of course that he has no claim on God's mercy because of these works). However, the man himself is actually sent to hell for one specific reason. John states, "And anyone not found written in the Book of Life was cast into the lake of fire" (v 15). We may say, therefore, that every human being is estranged from God—or, as Paul puts it, "alienated from *the life of God*, because of the ignorance that is in them, because of the blindness of their heart" (Eph 4:18, emphasis added). Unless such a man is reconciled personally to God by faith in Christ so that he partakes of *the life of God*, he faces the prospect of spending eternity in a place suitable for all who are estranged from their Maker. That is, in eternal hell.

Finally, we may add this: A lost person is not sentenced to hell for the sins Christ died for. Neither does he pay all over again for those sins. Instead, he reaps the consequences of his own estrangement from God. The deeper that estrangement is the more severe his experience of hell will no doubt be (see, for example, Matt 11:22, 24; Mark 6:11).

God never makes the sins of the world the grounds for man's eternal damnation. As a judicial issue, the Lamb of God has taken them away!

CHAPTER 2

The Risen Sacrificial Lamb

In our first section on *The Atonement*, we discussed the universal character of Christ's sacrificial work on the cross. We saw that the Scriptures teach that He died for all humanity, not just for the elect, and that this atonement was actual and not simply *potential*. As a result of His atoning work, God's justice regarding sin has been satisfied. On this basis, eternal life is offered to everyone who will receive it by faith.

Let us look again at one of the Biblical texts we considered last time. According to the Apostle John, our "Advocate with the Father" is "Jesus Christ the righteous." John declares of Him that "He *Himself* is the propitiation for our sins, and not for ours only but also for the whole world" (1 John 2:1-2, emphasis added).

Had we been writing these words, we might have been tempted to write them this way: "He Himself *made propitiation* for our sins." In this way we would have been referring to the work of the cross as an accomplished reality—which, of course, it is. However, John doesn't say it this way. Instead, He personalizes the propitiation by stating that He *Himself*—that is, Jesus Christ in His own Person—is that propitiation.

John's way of putting it reminds us of the truth that it is Jesus "who *Himself* bore our sins in His own body on the tree" (1 Pet 2:24, emphasis added). The Lord Jesus, therefore, did more than simply *offer* the sacrifice. He *is* the sacrifice. This precise point is strongly emphasized by the writer of Hebrews.

In a memorable affirmation, Hebrews declares of our Lord that "now, once at the end of the ages, He has appeared to *put away sin by the sacrifice of Himself*" (Heb 9:26, emphasis added). It follows then that Jesus Christ stands in dramatic contrast to every animal sacrifice offered under the Old Testament Law. The remains of every such animal had to be disposed of after the offering was made, since the animal remained dead. But in the case of Jesus Christ, the Lamb of God has been raised from the dead. His victory over death is complete and permanent. This marvelous triumph is expressed in our Lord's own words to the Apostle John: "I am He who lives, and was dead, and behold, I am alive forevermore. Amen" (Rev 1:18).

Therefore, as Jesus Christ stands today as our Advocate before God, God's gaze is focused upon *Him personally* as the all-sufficient propitiation for the sins of the world. *In His own Person* Jesus represents God's complete satisfaction with the work of the cross. God's approving eye rests *at all times* on His crucified, but risen, sacrificial Lamb. Thus, it is not surprising that in John's symbolic version of the heavenly throne room he sees "in the midst of the throne and of the four living creatures, and in the midst of the elders," that there "stood a Lamb as though it had been slain" (Rev 5:6).

The work of the cross, therefore, is complete, but our Lord's character as the Lamb who satisfies God's justice is eternal. So we cannot say, "He *was* the propitiation for the sins of the whole world." Instead, with God's word, we must say, "He *is* the propitiation!" Regardless of man's faith or unbelief, this reality is supremely unaffected: He is the *eternally effective* propitiation for the sins of all humanity.

With this in mind we can appreciate with greater clarity the significant words of the Apostle Paul who wrote:

> Now it was not written for his [Abraham's] sake alone that it [righteousness] was imputed to him, but also for us. It shall be imputed to us who believe in Him who raised up Jesus our Lord from the dead, who was delivered up because of our offenses, and was raised because of [or, for the sake of] our justification (Rom 4:23-25).

We note here how closely Paul connects the experience of justification by faith with the fact of our Lord's resurrection from the dead. His death itself was the execution of divine justice for our sins ("our offenses"). His resurrection, on the other hand, brings up from the dead, and ultimately into the presence of God, the Lamb who is personally the propitiation for the world's sins.

Another way of expressing this is that the sacrificial Lamb whose life was given up on the cross has returned to the presence of His Father in a new capacity. He is now the Lamb who was slain and bears the marks of His suffering in His resurrected physical body (see John 20:27). His Father not only receives Him back, but also exalts Him above every other being and gives Him a name above every other name (see Phil 2:5-11). God is supremely and eternally satisfied with His Son Jesus Christ.

Christians often speak as if the resurrection simply *verified* the effectiveness of the atoning work of our Savior from an earthly point of view. Of course, it does do this. However, the resurrection also means that God Himself now contemplates the Person of His Son as the all-sufficient *propitiation* for the entire world, and that every individual case of justification is predicated on His perfect satisfaction with His Son.

He was "raised for [the sake of] our justification" (Rom 4:25). Our justification rests on the Risen One who is now, and always, "the propitiation for our sins" (1 John 2:2).

So one may raise the question (as Paul does): "Who shall bring a charge against God's elect?" To this he replies, "It is God who justifies. Who is he who condemns?" There is no one who really can condemn. Why? Because "it is Christ who died, and furthermore is also risen, who is even at the right hand of God, who also makes intercession for us" (Rom 8:33-34). Clearly, this recapitulates the truth of 1 John 2:1-2 that our "Advocate with the Father" is personally the propitiation for our sins. In His own Person, as the One who died, rose, was received at God's right hand and who intercedes for us, He is the insuperable and impervious barrier to any and every charge against God's elect children.

God accepts Jesus Christ as the visible and personal expression of propitiation for all human sin—both ours and also the whole world's. How then can we be concerned with the adequacy of His propitiation for *us*? Our concern is groundless! So magnificent is His propitiatory role that He has also satisfied God about the sins of the entire human race. In terms of the justice demanded by the Judge of all, He is "the Lamb of God who takes away the sin of the world" (John 1:29).

So the grounds on which God regenerates and justifies the believer in Jesus are infinitely adequate. Or, as Paul puts it elsewhere: God is both "*just* and the *justifier* of the one who has faith in Jesus" (Rom 3:26, emphasis added). The risen Person of Jesus Christ is God's eternal *justification* for His gracious *justifying* of everyone who believes.

CHAPTER 3

The New Mercy Seat

As we have seen thus far, by his sacrifice on the cross the Lord Jesus Christ has become *in His own Person* the propitiation (satisfaction) for the sins of all humanity. Thus in His role as our Mediator in the presence of God, His Father sees Him as the One who has perfectly met the demands of divine justice against sin (1 John 2:2).

The concept of our Risen Lord standing before God as the propitiation for human sins reminds me of the Old Testament Holy of Holies. In that most sacred area (both in the Tabernacle and in the Temple) there stood the Ark of the Covenant over which was placed a golden slab known to us from our Bibles as the Mercy Seat. Out of either end of the Mercy Seat, as an integral part of it, came the figures of two cherubim. The faces of the cherubim were both looking at the Mercy Seat itself and the wings of the cherubim were spread out over the Mercy Seat (see Exod 25:17-22; 37:6-9).

On the Day of Atonement, of course, the High Priest brought sacrificial blood into the Holy of Holies and sprinkled it on the Mercy Seat (see Lev 16:1-17). Of particular importance is the statement, "So He shall make atonement for the Holy Place, because of the uncleanness of the children of Israel, and because of their transgressions, for all their sins" (Lev 16:16). But it is also important to observe the divine declaration that follows the command to construct the Mercy Seat. For God says of the Mercy Seat,

> You shall put the mercy seat on the top of the ark, and in the ark you shall put the Testimony that I will give you.

And there I will meet with you, and I will speak with you
from above the mercy seat, from between the two cherubim
which are on the ark of the Testimony, about everything
which I will give you in commandment to the children of
Israel (Exod 5:21-22, emphasis added).

The blood-sprinkled Mercy Seat was therefore a point of meeting
between God and man. In Exod 25:22 Moses is in view, but Lev 16:2
seems to imply that this could happen to Aaron (or even to his high
priestly descendants).

This understanding of the ritual background of the Mercy Seat
helps us to gain insight into a famous statement by the Apostle
Paul. In Rom 3:21-26 Paul is discussing the imputed "righteousness of God" which is offered "to all" but is actually bestowed "on
all who believe" (v 22). This of course is the truth of justification by
faith. Paul goes on to declare that men are "justified freely by His
grace through the redemption that is in Christ Jesus, *whom God
set forth as a propitiation by His blood, through faith…*" (vv 24-25,
emphasis added). The words given here in italics have caused much
discussion in the literature of Romans.

The word translated *propitiation* in Rom 3:25 is related to, but not
the same as, the word translated *propitiation* in 1 John 2:2. In Rom
3:25 the Apostle uses the word *hilasterion*.

This particular Greek word is primarily used in the Septuagint
(Greek Old Testament) to render the Hebrew word for Mercy
Seat (*kapporet*). It also means Mercy Seat in its only other New
Testament use in Heb 9:5. Thus it is very likely that in Rom 3:25 we
have this same meaning.

As I previously mentioned, the translation of the Greek word,
hilasterion, into the English, *Mercy Seat*, rather than the typical
propitiation, is key to understanding Paul's meaning in Rom 3:25.

In his commentary, *The Epistle to the Romans*, Douglas Moo
writes:

When the use of *hilasterion* in the Bible is considered, a
strong case can be made for taking the word as a reference
to the OT "mercy seat," the cover over the ark where [the
Lord] appeared (Lev. 16:2), and on which sacrificial blood
was poured.

He goes on to add:

By referring to Christ as this "mercy seat" then, Paul would be inviting us to view Christ as the New Covenant equivalent, or antitype, to the Old Covenant "place of atonement," and derivatively, to the ritual of atonement itself. What in the OT was hidden from view behind the veil has now been "publicly displayed" as the OT ritual is fulfilled and brought to an end in Christ's "once-for-all" sacrifice. This interpretation, which has an ancient and respectable heritage, has been gaining strength in recent years.[1]

This is very well said. Equally relevant is Moo's later remark that, "Christ, Paul implies, now has the place that the 'mercy seat' had in the Old Covenant, the center and focal point of God's provision of atonement for his people" (p. 236).

This interpretation is completely harmonious with what is covered in the first two chapters of this book. Christ in His own Person is the propitiation for all human sin. Now, in the light of our understanding of Rom 3:25, we can add a further observation. As a result of His becoming the living embodiment before God of a perfect and universal propitiation for all sin (1 John 2:2), in His own Person He is *also* a living "Mercy Seat." That is to say, He has also become an infinitely sufficient "meeting place" between a Holy God and a sinful man. In fact, as Paul indicates here, "God has set [Him] forth" as a Mercy Seat "*through faith*"!

Thus, when "faith in Jesus" (Rom 3:26) occurs, God and man encounter one another and the human recipient in this encounter is justified, receiving "the righteousness of God" that Paul is talking about. Accordingly, Jesus is "the way, the truth, and the life. No one comes to the Father except through" Him (John 14:6). Man meets God only by "faith in Jesus."

---

[1] Douglas J. Moo, *The Epistle to the Romans* (Grand Rapids, MI: William B. Eerdmans Publishing Company, 1996), 231-32.

CHAPTER 4

Through Faith in His Blood

As we saw in the previous chapter, Rom 3:25 presents our Lord Jesus Christ as the fulfillment of the Old Testament Mercy Seat. The Greek word for Mercy Seat (*hilasterion*), used in Rom 3:25, belongs to the family of words from which comes the Greek word for propitiation (*hilasmos*). In Old Testament times the Mercy Seat was sprinkled with sacrificial blood once a year on the Day of Atonement. It was also a place of encounter between man and God (Exod 25:21-22).

In fulfillment of this imagery under the Old Covenant, our Lord Jesus Christ Himself becomes the propitiation for the sins of all humanity (1 John 2:2) and thus (*by His blood*) He becomes also the "meeting place" for God and man. To make clearer the distinction between 1 John 2:2 and Rom 3:25, I might paraphrase the latter like this: *whom God has set forth as the propitiatory meeting place.*

The language Paul uses in Rom 3:25 expresses a fundamental NT truth: God and sinful man can encounter one another in peace only in the Person of His Son. As the Apostle elsewhere states, "For there is one God and one Mediator between God and men, the Man Christ Jesus, who gave Himself a ransom for all" (1 Tim 2:5-6). The Lord Himself said, "I am the way, the truth, and the life. No one comes to the Father except through Me" (John 14:6).

This brings us to an important phrase in Rom 3:25, the words *through faith*. As mentioned previously, the positioning of the words *through faith* in the rendering given above (the NKJV) does not strictly correspond to their position in the original Greek. The literal order is as follows: as a *propitiation through faith (in/by) His blood.*

The Greek word represented in the NKJV as *by* can also mean *in.* This has led some to think that Paul is speaking about "faith in His [Jesus'] blood." In fact this is the sense adopted by the NIV. However, there is major commentary support for the meaning reflected in the NKJV (*a propitiation by His blood*) and in the NASB (*a propitiation in His blood*). In particular it is pointed out that Paul never elsewhere makes the blood of Christ the object of faith. (See discussions in the commentaries of James D. G. Dunn and Douglas Moo.)

Instead we should connect the phrase with the word *propitiation* (= Mercy Seat) and translate it this way: *a propitiation…by means of His blood.* The NKJV has simply altered the word order for the sake of clarity, as has the NASB.

Without at all criticizing the choice of word order by NKJV and NASB, it nevertheless remains true that the Greek word order is significant. Paul is basically connecting the words *through faith* with the word for Mercy Seat (*hilasterion*). That is to say, Jesus Christ becomes the New Covenant equivalent of the Mercy Seat *through faith.*

The point we are about to make is obscured by the English translations which use propitiation as a rendering for *hilasterion* here and also for *hilasmos* in 1 John 2:2. However, 1 John 2:2 is an unqualified assertion that the Son of God is "the propitiation for our sins, and not for ours only but also for the whole world." There is no qualification that He is this only if and when there is faith. The *whole world* is covered by His grand propitiatory work, whether they believe it or not.

However, that is not true in regard to our Lord's role as the fulfillment of the Mercy Seat. On the contrary, this mediatorial function is realized only when men come to God *through faith* in Jesus. Thus the saving encounter between man and God through the one and only Mediator is always, and only, an encounter that faith makes possible. The Lord Jesus Christ becomes a Mercy Seat *to those who believe.*

In Greek, the words that immediately follow the phrase *though faith* are the words *by His blood* (Rom 3:25). These words therefore give the basis on which our Lord Jesus Christ can be a Mercy Seat through faith. He can do so by virtue of His shed blood. In other words He can become the *hilasterion through faith* as a result of the fact that He is the *hilasmos* for the sins of all humanity.

This distinction is lost in our English translations, which employ the word "propitiation" in both Rom 3:25 and 1 John 2:2. Even though the different words in these passages are obviously related, the distinction between them is theologically significant. But in all fairness to the English translators, it is very difficult to find a satisfactory equivalent for *hilasterion* in Rom 3:25, unless we fall back on the words "Mercy Seat." However, a case can be made that this should have been done.

Let us pinpoint what we are saying. To be sure, our Lord is, and always will be, the one Mediator between man and God (1 Tim 2:5). So *hilasterion* in Rom 3:25 does not so much describe a *position* as it does a *function*. But we may also say this: whenever an unsaved sinner comes to God through God's chosen Mediator, Jesus fulfills the function of the Old Covenant Mercy Seat by becoming the genuine meeting point between God and the believing sinner.

In other words, man and God *really meet* in Jesus Christ when saving faith occurs. Unlike the inanimate Mercy Seat of Moses' day, the risen and living Jesus Christ "introduces" the sinner to God. And He does so by bestowing eternal life—God's life—on the one who believes, so that the believer knows God (see John 17:3). God on His part bestows His perfect righteousness on the believer.

One final point should be noted. Frequently, eternal life is presented as the bestowal of our Lord Jesus Christ Himself (see John 1:12; 4:10, 14; 6:27, 33; 10:38; 17:2). By contrast, the Son is never said to be the One who grants justification. Instead it is always "God who justifies" (Rom 8:33). Although the Persons in the Godhead are equal in essence and glory, their differing roles must always be noted.

Perhaps we might illustrate the saving transaction as follows (although so sublime an experience is really beyond our capacity to describe since it is experientially instantaneous): the believing sinner comes to God through faith in Jesus. Jesus in his role as Mediator bestows eternal life on the believer, thus introducing Him to God. God in response accepts the believing sinner and pronounces him justified.

What has happened to the believer? He has met God in the Person of God's living Mercy Seat, our Lord and Savior Jesus Christ.

And, what has God done? He has behaved righteously and graciously in response to His Son. Thus He has been "just and the justifier of the one who has faith in Jesus" (Rom 3:26).

CHAPTER 5

What Do We Mean by Propitiation?
Does It Only Count If We Accept It?[1]

H ave you ever heard an illustration like this? A man is spending his last week on death row. Suddenly the warden appears and shows him a piece of paper. The paper is a full pardon signed by the Governor. After the man looks it over, he says, "I don't want it." He hands it back to the warden. The illustration ends with the execution of the condemned man.

What's wrong with this story? Well, to begin with, there is no way a state would execute a pardoned man. The prisoner would be ushered unceremoniously out of his cell—at least eventually, depending on legal technicalities. Yet users of such an illustration think it is a good one. If human beings reject the pardon Jesus Christ bought for them by His death on the cross, they will go to hell and pay for their sins.

Can this be true? No, it cannot.

Jesus, Our Propitiation

The illustration above cannot be correct. The reason is that it denies the reality of the propitiation that the Lord Jesus Christ made on the cross. An expected objection must be confronted. Someone might argue this way: "The propitiation that Jesus made on the cross is

---

[1] This chapter was not originally part of *The Atonement* booklet. But since it further clarifies Hodges's views, we have included it here. It originally appeared in *JOTGES* (Spring 2006): 35-42.

real. It is fully adequate for all men. However, it is only effective if men believe it."

This view leads to a new illustration. A man deposits one billion dollars in the bank. Any debtor can come and draw freely on the account. It is sufficient to meet his needs. If he doesn't draw on it, the account does not pay for his debt. *He* has to pay for it.

What's wrong with *this* story? The same thing as before. It denies the reality of the propitiation that Jesus made on the cross. Nothing has really been paid for.

Such illustrations fly into the face of the Word of God. Listen to the words of the Apostle John in 1 John 2:2, referring to Jesus Christ: "And He Himself is the propitiation for our sins, and not for ours only but also for the whole world."

The Greek word translated "propitiation" (*hilasmos*) means either "appeasement necessitated by sin" or "expiation."[2] The long-running debate centering on the difference between "appeasement" and "expiation" can be ignored. It does not really make a difference to this discussion.

The word "appeasement," or the softer term "satisfaction," are each acceptable here. The concept of propitiation refers to something that appeases, or satisfies, the righteous justice of God. The word "satisfaction" is a pretty good equivalent.

But is there anything in 1 John 2:2 about Jesus Christ being *potentially* the "satisfaction" for the sins of the world? No, there is not. The Apostle flatly states that Jesus *is the propitiation* for the sins of "the whole world." He *is* that. Not that He *can* be, or *potentially* is, but He simply *is*. Note, too, that this statement is exactly parallel to the truth that He is the propitiation for *our* sins. In whatever sense He is the propitiation for our sins, He is also the propitiation for the sins of the whole world.

Very simply put, the propitiatory work of our Lord Jesus Christ is *universally* effective. That is true whether anyone believes it or not. On the cross, Jesus paid for every single sin that has ever been committed by any person who has ever lived on the face of the earth. That is magnificent and overwhelming!

---

[2] *A Greek-English Lexicon of the New Testament and Other Early Christian Literature*, ed. Frederick William Danker, 3rd ed. (Chicago/London: University of Chicago Press, 2000), 474.

Of course, the same truth is stated by the Apostle Paul in 2 Cor 5:19 where he writes, "God was in Christ reconciling the world to Himself, not imputing their trespasses to them..." At the cross, God imputed the sins of the *entire world* to Jesus Christ and did *not* impute them to the world.

Paul also expresses this truth in 1 Tim 2:5-6: "For there is one God and one Mediator between God and men, the *Man Christ Jesus, who gave Himself a ransom for all, to be testified in due time*" (emphasis added). Again, in whatever sense He is a ransom for us, He is a ransom *for all.*

For the same reason, John the Baptist declared in John 1:29: "Behold! The Lamb of God who takes away the sin of the world."

Unfortunately, many Christians do not understand the splendid universal sufficiency of the work of Christ on the cross. They frequently misrepresent it when they evangelize the unconverted. Fortunately, one does not have to have a perfect understanding of the cross to be saved. If that were the case, probably no one would be saved.

Propitiation and Final Judgment

At this point, someone will ask, "But how can God send anybody to hell if Jesus paid for all their sins on the cross?" Good question. In fact, so good that it is a shame that grace people haven't tried very often to answer it clearly.

Reformed people, however, have faced this issue and have an answer of their own. In their view, if Christ died for all of a man's sins, then that man can't be sent to hell. Therefore, he must be among the elect. This leads directly to the conclusion that Christ really died only for the elect.

This is the doctrine of limited atonement. Christ did not die *effectively* for the sins of all humanity. The key word, of course, is *effectively.* In some sense, a Reformed person might suggest, the cross may be viewed as sufficient for all, but effective only for the elect. Obviously, the Reformed answer is inadequate for grace people. But what should our answer be like? Let me state it and then try to support it.

Here it is: Since Christ effectively died for the sins of the entire world, nobody goes to hell for their sins. They go to hell because they do not have eternal life. This suggested answer is confirmed by the Biblical account of the final judgment found in Rev 20:11-15.

The first thing that strikes us about this account is that there is no mention of sin. That is very important: *there is no mention of sin in Rev 20:11-15.*

Of course, there *is* mention of men's works. Revelation 20:12 states, "And I saw the dead, small and great, standing before God, and books were opened. And another book was opened, which is the Book of Life. And the dead were judged according to their works, by the things which were written in the books." Clearly the things men have done in their lives—their works—are reviewed at the Great White Throne Judgment. This is both natural and very much to be expected.

Countless human beings have gone out into eternity convinced that their works will make them acceptable to God on the Day of Judgment. They are wrong, of course. Paul makes this plain in Romans and Galatians.[3] But many people are still convinced, to the day of their death, that the deciding issue will be their works. They hope that their good works will outweigh their bad works. They hope that God's verdict on their works will result in them going to heaven.

Naturally, God will not ignore this issue in the final judgment. That would be like a judge on earth refusing to hear evidence that a defendant thought would help him. Everything that any man or woman has ever done will be reviewed at the Great White Throne.

Interestingly enough, Revelation 20 does not state the result of this review. But the Book of Revelation was written to Christian churches that already knew what the result would be. Anyone who understands God's plan of salvation also knows that the result of such a review will be negative. It will reinforce the testimony of Scripture that "by the deeds of the law no flesh will be justified in His sight" (Rom 3:20).

To be sure, a review of anyone's works will involve looking at his or her sins. But at the Great White Throne, the issue will not be sins as such, but works, both good and bad. And even so, notice one important fact. Men are not condemned to hell even on the basis of their works.

---

[3] For example, Rom 4:5; 11:6; Gal 2:16.

As the text of Revelation makes clear, there is another book opened at the Great White Throne. It is the Book of Life. But this book is consulted only after the review of men's works based on the *other* books. Yet when it is consulted, its verdict is clear. We are told, "And anyone not found written in the Book of Life was cast into the lake of fire" (Rev 20:15).

Men do not go to hell because of their sins or their wicked works. They go to hell because their names are not found in the Book of Life. They do not have eternal life.

Where Do You Send the Unrighteous?

We all understand that human beings suffer the consequences of their sinful conduct while on earth. Trouble, sickness, rejection and dozens of other experiences—including physical death—are included in the ways in which sinners suffer these consequences.

We often call this the law of sowing and reaping. Paul tells us (Gal 6:7) that "whatever a man sows, that he will also reap." God has built this law into human experience. As long as a man remains a sinner he is subject to this unchanging law.

Christians are also subject to the law of sowing and reaping. Paul makes that clear in Gal 6:7-8. He tells the Galatians, "Do not be deceived, God is not mocked; for whatever a man sows, that he will also reap. For he who sows to his flesh will of the flesh reap corruption, but he who sows to the Spirit will of the Spirit reap everlasting life."

When any man, including a believer, lives sinfully and thereby sows to his flesh, he reaps corruption. Paul insists on that. But a believer has another option. He can also sow to the Spirit and reap an enrichment of his experience of eternal life. This last fact is important, but only the first part of the statement is pertinent to this article.

Sowing to the flesh produces corruption, no matter who does it. The death of Christ *does not affect this law*, either for the believer or the nonbeliever. This fact is very important. The word Paul uses for corruption in Gal 6:8 is the Greek word *phthora*, which fundamentally refers to "the breakdown of organic matter."[4]

---

[4] BDAG, 1054.

By extension it can refer to moral or spiritual ruin or decay of one kind or another.

The Lord Jesus Christ spoke more often about hell than any person in the New Testament. In one of His most striking discussions of hell, He described it in terms of *corruption*. Mark 9:45-46 illustrates this:

> And if your foot causes your downfall, cut it off. It is better for you to enter life lame, than having two feet, to be cast into Gehenna into the fire that shall never be quenched— where their worm does not die and the fire is not quenched (author's translation).

This memorable description vividly describes a scene of decay and ruin. In Gehenna there is an endlessly burning fire and there are worms whose activity is unceasing. Gehenna, or hell, may be described as a place of *eternal corruption*.

We may think of hell, therefore, as an extension of the law of sowing and reaping. Those who go there are reaping eternal *corruption* . In fact, it is the only suitable place to put unsaved sinners. It is the only place that suitably fits their sinful nature and character.

Hell is justified, therefore, because its inhabitants do not share God's kind of life. They do not have eternal life and, as a result, they cannot live with Him. Instead, they must endure everlasting corruption.

The cross of Christ eliminated sin as the grounds for *judicial condemnation*. It satisfied God's righteous demand for a *judicial* punishment for human sin. It made possible the justification and new birth of all who believe. As Paul puts it so beautifully in Rom 3:26, God can now be "just and the justifier of the one who has faith in Jesus."

In all cultures that I am aware of, there is a distinction made between natural or circumstantial retribution and judicial retribution. This can be easily illustrated.

Here is a man who has long been a drug dealer. One day, in a drug war he is shot and killed. This is clearly a consequence of his drug dealing ways. But it is a natural consequence in the sense that circumstances led to it. On the other hand, he might be arrested and sentenced to death for murdering another dealer. When he is executed, he is suffering the *judicial* consequences of his drug dealing.

The distinction that has just been made is perfectly natural and quite common whenever we talk about consequences. At the cross, Jesus Christ suffered the punishment that God, the Judge of all men, demands for sin. It cannot ever be paid again. No one will ever suffer a *judicial* punishment for sin, because Jesus paid that.

The suffering that Christ endured on the cross was excruciatingly painful, both physically and emotionally. But what He suffered is enough to remove *judicial* punishment from all humanity for all time.

In the following illustration, please don't hold me to a strict literal sense. The illustration is suggestive and thought provoking. Please take it that way.

> Going to hell is like being marooned on a rotting boat that is going in circles on a sea of boiling water. That is the natural, future consequence of human sin. The judicial consequence would be like being on the same boat but chained to the oars night and day, compelled to row the boat without letup or relief. The first is dreadful enough. The second is far worse.

What is the bottom line? It is this: Men are not sent to hell for their sins. They are sent there because they are not listed in the Book of Life. But the death of Christ does not cancel the law of sowing and reaping. When people who are dead in trespasses and sins go to hell, they are *eternally* reaping what they have sowed.

Hell was originally prepared for the devil and his angels as stated in Matt 25:41. But hell is the only appropriate place to send unregenerate people who die in their sins. As Jesus said in John 8:24, "If you do not believe that I am He, you will die in your sins."

Corruption and Life

Perhaps you noticed in Gal 6:7-8 that the Apostle Paul contrasts *corruption* with *everlasting life*. The Lord Jesus does the same thing in Mark 9:45-46. There He states that "it is better to enter *life* lame, than…to be cast into Gehenna…where their worm does not die."

Both Jesus and Paul set *life* and *corruption* before us as opposites. Of course, for the believer here and now there is the potential experience of both things, depending on where he sows—whether to the flesh or to the Spirit. But this, of course, is due to the fact that the believer's inward nature is regenerate and his body still awaits transformation.

However, the believer yearns for his eternal body as Paul tells us in 2 Cor 5:1-4. Paul's words are vivid: "For we who are in this tent groan, being burdened, not because we want to be unclothed, but further clothed, that mortality may be swallowed up by life" (2 Cor 5:4).

Just a little earlier (2 Cor 4:16), Paul had stated that "our outward man is perishing, yet the inward man is being renewed day by day." In other words, we have eternal life within us, but our physical body is subject to corruption and death.

When the Lord comes, however, our bodies will be changed so that they can fully express the *life* within us. At that point, our "mortality," Paul says, will be "swallowed up by *life*." From then on, we will no longer experience *corruption*. Our whole experience will be that of *eternal life*.

What about the unregenerate person? When *he* is raised from the dead to stand at the Great White Throne, his body will *still* be untransformed. It will still be an appropriate habitation for his equally untransformed inward man. Where then should such a person be sent?

The unsaved man cannot enter into life, since he has no divine life within him. Thus he must be put into the one habitat that is suitable for him. That is Gehenna, where "the fire shall never be quenched" and "where their worm does not die." The spiritually dead sinner is cast into "the lake of fire" (Rev 20:15) where he continues to reap unending *corruption*.

Lacking eternal life, his doom in Gehenna is sealed. At the Great White Throne he can claim nothing based on his works. And when his name is not found written in the Book of Life, the lake of fire is his only possible destination.

Hell is the inevitable consequence of remaining *dead* in trespasses and sins. This deadness leads first to the death of our physical bodies, and then to the second death, as well. That is, it leads to the lake of fire (Rev 20:14).

Conclusion

It is hoped that the result of this brief article will be to magnify our view of the cross of Christ. So splendid is the propitiation accomplished at the cross, that every human being that has ever lived is freed from judicial condemnation for his or her sins.

When we sing, "Jesus paid it all," we mean it. God does not exact from any man the judicial penalty that Jesus paid at the cross. Jesus Christ's completely sufficient suffering on the cross for the sins of the world will never be repeated in the case of any human being whatsoever.

Furthermore, as a result of the cross, every man or woman is eligible for the free gift of eternal life. All they need to do is believe in Jesus for that gift. But those who do not believe remain dead in their sins and subject to the corruption that sin always brings. Though eligible for life, they have remained in spiritual death. Hell is the consequence of remaining dead to God.

In hell the law of sowing and reaping goes on and on and on. The fire is never put out and the worms of corruption never die. In hell, the superlative gift of life, paid for by our Savior's blood, has been missed forever. But that splendid gift is for everybody, for the simple reason that Christ died for everybody equally.

That's wonderful! Let's get out there and tell people about this.

CHAPTER 6

The Sin of Unbelief[1]

S ometimes grace people do not think as clearly as they need to on important issues. The sin of unbelief—not believing in the Lord Jesus Christ for eternal life—is one of these issues. Let me address some questions that have, or might, arise on this subject.

Q: Did Christ die for the sin of unbelief?
A: Of course. He died for all the sins of all mankind (1 John 2:2).

Q: Then why does God send people to hell for not believing?
A: He doesn't. The Bible nowhere says that.

Q: Then what does He send them to hell for?
A: For not having their names in the Book of Life (Rev 20:15).

Q: But isn't that because they didn't believe?
A: Yes. But it's still not the reason they are condemned to hell.

Q: Isn't that double-talk?
A: Not at all. A cause and a reason are not the same thing. Unbelief is the cause for the unsaved not having eternal life. Not having eternal life is the reason they are condemned to hell.

Let's say a man on parole is required to be in his home by 11:00 pm. One night he is visiting his aunt and stays there until midnight.

---

[1] This chapter was not originally part of *The Atonement* booklet. But since it further clarifies Hodges's views, we have included it here. It originally appeared in *Grace in Focus* (Nov-Dec. 2007): 2-3.

His violation is discovered and he is sent back to prison. Why? Was it because he had a long visit with his aunt? No, not really. It was because he fell below the required standard for his parole. The visit with the aunt was the effective cause of the violation, but the violation of parole itself was the legal reason he is returned to prison.

When this man returns to prison the legal decision on which this fact is based will not require the state to make reference to his visit to his aunt! He simply violated parole.

At the Great White Throne Judgment (Rev 20:11-15) people are temporarily released (paroled!) from hell (Hades) and the issue of their permanent eternal abode becomes a legal matter in the presence of their Judge (Jesus Christ: John 5:22). They are first judged according to their works to see if these works justify their permanent release from eternal judgment (Rev 20:13). As we know, there will be no justification based on works (Rom 3:20). Next, search is made in the Book of Life to see if they qualify for release because they have eternal life. They do not and are therefore placed in an eternal abode (the Lake of Fire) in separation from their Judge forever.

Although the outcome of this whole process is a foregone conclusion, the justice of God requires the process to take place. Even in our own society, a man caught red-handed in the act of murder (or some other crime) must have his day in court. Every unsaved person will have his or her day in God's court.

In this whole process, the Scripture text makes no reference at all to sin as such, but instead refers first to works (Rev 20:13), and next to life (Rev 20:15). Sin, as such, has no place as a determining factor at this judgment.

Why is that? It is because the Judge (Jesus Christ) is also the Lamb of God who has taken away the sin of the world (John 1:29). The Judge will not bring up an issue that He Himself has dealt with on the cross. This Judge will condemn no human being whatsoever for any sin whatsoever.

He has taken all that away.

Part II
Did Paul Preach Eternal Life? Should We?

Foreword

In Homer's great epic poem called *The Odyssey,* it is recounted how on his homeward voyage Odysseus had to sail by the Isle of the Sirens. The Sirens were a group of sea nymphs whose beautiful singing lured mariners to destruction on the rocks of their island.

To get safely past the island, Odysseus plugged the ears of his sailors with beeswax so they could not hear the Sirens' music. But since he himself wanted to listen to their lovely singing, he had his crew stand him by the step of his ship's mast, bind him hand and foot with rope and lash him to the mast.

Only in this way did he and his crew pass safely beyond the range of these alluring voices.

Today many evangelicals listen to the Siren song of what is now called postmodernism. The song sung by postmodern voices is a call to diversity and variety, whether social, sexual, philosophical, or religious. No single statement of truth is to be preferred to some other statement, and the concept of absolute truth is severely disparaged.

Tragically, some who profess to hold the Biblical doctrine of God's saving grace have argued that this doctrine can be couched in a variety of ways. No single articulation of the gospel should be given primacy over any other. A diversity of messages to the lost is not to be deplored, but rather can be warmly approved.

But this point of view is an invitation to doctrinal shipwreck. To listen to its alluring music is to go off course and head for the rocks of theological confusion and error. The only way to avoid such a calamity is to lash ourselves to the solid mast of divine revelation, or to stop our ears by filling them with God's truth.

This section is an effort to do that. In it I affirm that the Biblical gospel of God's saving grace is not a postmodern religious smorgasbord. Instead it is a divine revelation by which all other so-called "gospels" must be held to account.

Introduction

Unending life, resurrection, and eternal participation in the world to come—all of these are the heritage of every born again believer in Jesus Christ.

But did the Apostle Paul preach this truth? Did Paul preach eternal life? Was everlasting life the core of His gospel?

It seems almost ridiculous to ask this question. The Lord Jesus Christ made eternal life the very core and essence of His gospel. This is perfectly plain from many passages in the Gospel of John (see 3:15, 16; 4:14; 5:24; 6:27, 40, 54; 10:28; 17:2, 3). But if Jesus did this, so surely must the Apostle Paul have done so. After all, by his own account, Paul received his gospel directly from Jesus Christ. In Gal 1:11-12 Paul wrote:

> But I make known to you, brethren, that the gospel which was preached by me is not according to man. For I neither received it from man, nor was I taught it, but it came through the revelation of Jesus Christ.

Of course, Paul is speaking of his encounter with our Lord on the road to Damascus. The gospel that Paul subsequently proclaimed came directly from the Son of God. And the gospel that Jesus Himself preached centered on eternal life.

It is therefore illogical to think that Paul did not proclaim a gospel that was the same as the message Jesus gave to men.

Yet in our own day this simple truth has been questioned. We live in a postmodern age that celebrates diversity, whether ethnic, social, sexual, political, or theological. It is not surprising that some evangelicals think that there is significant diversity in the gospel message. According to them, the gospel can be presented in a variety of ways that need not be closely harmonized with one another.

As a result, some have even suggested that Paul preached a gospel in which eternal life did not need to be mentioned at all. Instead it was adequate (according to this view) to preach "forgiveness of sins" or "justification," or simply "salvation" in some unspecified sense.

Such a view reflects serious doctrinal confusion about the nature of the NT gospel. It obscures the basic truth which the gospel of God's Son was intended to convey. And it drives a wedge between the message of Paul and the message of his Lord.

CHAPTER 7

Paul's Gospel Message

When Paul reflected on his own conversion, he thought of eternal life. This is plain from a famous text in 1 Tim 1:15-16. In that passage he writes:

> This is a faithful saying and worthy of all acceptance, that Christ Jesus came into the world to save sinners, of whom I am chief. However, for this reason I obtained mercy, that in me first Jesus Christ might show all longsuffering, as a pattern to those who are going to believe on Him for everlasting life.

My conversion, Paul is saying, *is a pattern for all conversions to follow. I am the ideal example of the salvation of sinners.* And what were Paul and those who came after him called upon to believe? Paul's answer is simple: those who came after him (and who thus followed his example) were "to believe on Him [that is, Jesus Christ] for everlasting life."

In the book of Acts, Luke records what we refer to as Paul's first missionary journey. His account makes clear that the message of Paul (and Barnabas) centered on the issue of eternal life. Following Paul's speech in the synagogue of Antioch, he recounts the appeal made by the Gentiles that "these words might be preached to them the next Sabbath" (Acts 13:42). The Gentiles wanted to hear the *same message.*

The following Sabbath "almost the whole city came together to hear the word of God" (Acts 13:44).

This large audience provoked the envy of the Jews so that they were "contradicting and blaspheming" while they "opposed the things spoken by Paul" (13:45).

What exactly did they oppose? Acts 13:46 tells us:

> Then Paul and Barnabas grew bold and said, "It was necessary that the word of God should be spoken to you first; but since you reject it, and judge yourselves unworthy of *everlasting life*, behold, we turn to the Gentiles" (emphasis added).

In other words it was *everlasting life* that the unbelieving Jews were rejecting. They refused to believe on Jesus Christ for *everlasting life* as Paul had done at his conversion on the Damascus road. Ironically, Paul states that—in effect—they had judged themselves to be "unworthy" of this superlative life that they were spurning.

But in turning to the Gentiles with the very message that the Jews refused to believe, Paul and Barnabas were fulfilling Scripture. Thus Paul goes on to say in Acts 13:47:

> For so the Lord has commanded us: "I have set you as a light to the Gentiles, that you should be for *salvation* to the ends of the earth" (emphasis added).

Luke's final comment on this scene in Antioch of Pisidia is incisive. In Acts 13:48 he wraps up his account of Paul's evangelism there with the words:

> Now when the Gentiles heard this, they were glad and glorified the word of the Lord. And as many as had been appointed to *eternal life* believed (emphasis added).

All of this is quite clear. When Paul preached *salvation* to both the Jews and the Gentiles, he was preaching *eternal life*.

CHAPTER 8

The Synagogue Sermon

The sermon that Paul gave in the synagogue of Antioch in Pisidia covers a mere 26 verses in the book of Acts. We can read it in its entirety inside of five minutes. It would be foolish to claim that Paul's actual sermon only lasted several minutes.

What we clearly have in Acts 13:16-41 is Luke's *condensation* of Paul's message. That means that Paul said *a lot more* than Luke records. Needless to say, in writing a book like Acts, the author necessarily shortens the speeches so that they fit within the framework of his book. This does not mean that they are inaccurate. A condensation skillfully done can be perfectly accurate and true to the original speech.

It is noteworthy that in this *first evangelistic speech* by Paul in Acts, Luke includes a reference to forgiveness and to justification. (This latter concept only occurs here in Acts 13:39.) So we read that Paul said:

> Therefore let it be known to you, brethren, that through this Man is preached to you the forgiveness of sins; and by Him everyone who believes is justified from all things from which you could not be justified by the law of Moses (Acts 13:38-39).

As Paul clearly states here, every believer in Jesus Christ receives the forgiveness of sins and is justified at the moment of faith. But does Paul's statement (as reported by Luke) mean that Paul *did not even mention* eternal life in the speech itself?

That conclusion would be absurd in the light of the subsequent verses we have just looked at (13:42, 44-48). Paul had pointed out to his mainly Jewish audience that he was bringing them "the word of this salvation" (13:26). The term "salvation" is picked up again, as we just saw, in 13:47 in immediate connection with the reference to everlasting life in 13:46. And in the verse that follows the reference to salvation, eternal life is again mentioned (13:48).

It would strain all credulity to suggest that nowhere in the synagogue speech did Paul actually mention eternal life. Salvation and eternal life are unmistakably linked in Acts 13:46-48, just as they are in 1 Tim 1:15-16.

Clearly, in Acts, we have a skillful author at work. His condensation of Paul's speech does not contain the crucial term *eternal life* precisely because he wishes to reserve this pivotal phrase for the climactic section in Acts 13:42-52. It is the fundamental, pivotal term in the Pauline gospel of salvation, as is evident also in 1 Tim 1:15-16.

CHAPTER 9

Life and Salvation

W̶e have just seen that in Pauline thought eternal life and salvation belong together. This is plain from the two texts previously examined.

In 1 Tim 1:15-16, Paul tells us that "Christ Jesus came into the world to save sinners" and that sinners are saved when they "believe on Him for eternal life." In Acts 13:47, Paul and Barnabas declare that "salvation" is for the Gentiles, and Luke immediately informs us how salvation occurred on that occasion when "as many as were appointed to eternal life believed."

One cannot separate eternal life and salvation without destroying their close connection in Paul's gospel. Paul is an Apostle of Jesus Christ who declared, "Most assuredly, I say to you, he who believes in Me has everlasting life" (John 6:47).

That was Paul's message too. To ignore this fact, or deny it, is to fall prey to doctrinal confusion. The result is a view of the gospel that is more postmodern than Biblical.

The vital connection between life and salvation is strongly affirmed elsewhere as well. A classic passage is found in Ephesians 2.

In Eph 2:1-3, Paul describes the spiritual condition of his readers in the days when they were unconverted. He reminds them that they were at that time "dead in trespasses and sins" (v 1). They lived therefore under the influence of Satan and they fulfilled "the desires of the flesh and of the mind" (vv 2-3). In this *dead* spiritual condition they were "by nature children of wrath" (v 3b).

But salvation radically changed this dead condition. In vv 4-5 Paul states:

But God, who is rich in mercy, because of His great love with which He loved us, even when we were dead in trespasses, *made us alive* together with Christ (by grace you have been *saved*)...(emphasis added).

What then did the Ephesian believers receive when they got saved? They got exactly what they needed most—new life.

CHAPTER 10

Rebirth (Titus 3:4-7)

S alvation and eternal life are equally indissoluble in Titus 3:4-7. Paul says:

> But when the kindness and the love of God our Savior toward man appeared, not by works of righteousness which we have done, but according to His mercy He *saved* us, through the washing of *regeneration* and renewing of the Holy Spirit, whom He poured out on us abundantly through Jesus Christ our Savior, that having been justified by His grace we should become heirs according to the hope of *eternal life* (emphasis added).

This is an impressive catalogue of the benefits of salvation. But here we must primarily notice that Paul's statement about these benefits *begins and ends* with a reference to *eternal life*.

"God our Savior" has "saved us," Paul affirms, "through the washing of regeneration." The original Greek word translated "regeneration" (*palingenesia*) basically means "rebirth." It is linguistically composed of a prefix meaning "again" (*palin*) and a root referring to "birth" (*genesis*). The same root is also found in the word for "birthday celebration" (*genesia*). Paul is talking in Titus 3:5 about new birth.

Unmistakably Paul's word "regeneration" echoes our Lord's own teaching, expressed to Nicodemus in John 3:7, "Do not marvel that I said to you, 'You must be born again.'"

Following the reference to new birth, Paul also mentions the blessing of the "renewing of the Holy Spirit, whom He poured out on us abundantly" (Titus 3:5b-6). This is the gift of the Spirit that believers since Pentecost have been privileged to receive in addition to new life (see John 7:39). Moreover, Paul also adds a reference here to the fact that a saved person is "justified by His grace," a truth Paul expounds at length in Romans 3 and 4 (and to which we will return shortly).

New birth—the gift of the Spirit—justification by grace—such are the benefits bestowed on those whom God has saved, "not by works...but according to His mercy" (v 5). But the final, climactic benefit is expressed in the words "that...we should become heirs according to the hope of eternal life" (v 7).

The word "hope" should not be understood here in the sense of something dubious or uncertain. Instead the Greek word (*elpis*) ought to be rendered in this text by the term "expectation." The person who has been regenerated is an heir. He has an inheritance that is part and parcel of his expectation of unending, everlasting life. What is that? Very simply it is the resurrection and immortality that are guaranteed to every born again believer.

Paul speaks often of this truth. He communicates it vividly in 1 Cor 15:51-52:

> Behold, I tell you a mystery: We shall not all sleep, but we shall all be changed—in a moment, in the twinkling of an eye, at the last trumpet. For the trumpet will sound, and the dead will be raised incorruptible, and we shall be changed.

Equally impressive are his words in Phil 3:20-21:

> For our citizenship is in heaven, from which we also eagerly wait for the Savior, the Lord Jesus Christ, who will transform our lowly body that it may be conformed to His glorious body, according to the working by which He is able even to subdue all things to Himself.

But let it also be clearly recalled that the expectation of resurrection and of immortal, glorified life is a guarantee rooted deeply in the gospel of Jesus Christ Himself. In fact, in John 6:38-39, Jesus personally made this guarantee:

> For I have come down from heaven, not to do my own will, but the will of Him who sent Me. This is the will of the

Father who sent Me, that of all He has given Me I should lose nothing, but should raise it up at the last day.

Immediately after saying this, Jesus repeats the same guarantee (v 40):

And this is the will of Him who sent Me, that everyone who sees the Son and believes in Him may have everlasting life; and I will raise him up at the last day.

It should be plain that all believers, without exception, are "heirs according to the expectation of eternal life." Their assured destiny is to *inherit* a resurrected physical body and "eternal glory" (2 Tim 2:10). Though not all of us will "sleep" (in death), "we shall all be changed in a moment, in the twinkling of an eye." This is indeed a superlative inheritance and it is made possible by the miraculous event of *new birth* that brings us into possession of *eternal life*.

Accordingly, Paul's grand statement in Titus 3:4-7, about the benefits of salvation, is bounded (front and back) by references to eternal life. Salvation initially brings us eternal life at the moment of *regeneration* and that life, in turn, guarantees that we shall *inherit* physical immortality.

CHAPTER 11

Evangelizing (Acts 16:31)

In the career of Paul, as recorded in Acts, the most famous case of personal evangelism is the story of the conversion of the Philippian jailer (Acts 16:16-34). In that familiar story, Paul and Silas are arrested for casting a demon out of a slave girl who followed them crying, "These men are the servants of the Most High God, who proclaim to us the way of *salvation*" (Acts 16:17).

True though her words were, God does not want the testimony of demons. But after the girl's demon was cast out, her owners railroaded Paul and Silas into the local prison. It was there that God gave them an impressive opportunity to evangelize a Philippian jailer.

The story has been told countless times in Sunday school classes as well as from pulpits. Its facts are familiar. When an earthquake shook the jail in which Paul and Silas were being held, opening all the doors and shaking loose all the prisoners' chains (16:26), the following encounter took place:

> And the keeper of the prison, awaking from sleep and seeing the prison doors open, supposing the prisoners had fled, drew his sword and was about to kill himself. But Paul called with a loud voice, saying, "Do yourself no harm, for we are all here." Then he called for a light, ran in, and fell down trembling before Paul and Silas. And he brought them out and said, "Sirs, what must I do to be saved?" So they said, "Believe on the Lord Jesus Christ, and you will be saved, you and your household." Then [Greek = And] they

spoke the word of the Lord to him, and to all who were in his house (Acts 16:27-32).

As simple as this story is, it is sometimes handled in a totally irresponsible way. Some have wished to assign to the word saved here a meaning that they themselves prefer rather than the meaning intended by Paul and Silas—and by Luke himself.

Any person who reads Acts 16:31 and ignores the Pauline theology found in Acts 13 is guilty of gross interpretive negligence. In Acts 13:16-49 Luke is at pains to set before us Paul's fundamental message of salvation. As in Paul's epistles, this message is inseparably linked to the offer of eternal life to sinners. We have only ourselves to blame if we forget that here.

Putting it simply, the salvation that is offered to the Philippian jailer is nothing less than the offer of eternal life. To be saved, in Pauline theology, is to be *made alive* in Christ Jesus (Eph 2:4-9).

Someone may wish to ask, "But how was the Philippian jailor supposed to know this?" The answer is that Paul explained it to him. That was the only way he *could* have known.

If we take Acts 16:31 all by itself and imagine (falsely) that nothing else was said, *how was the Philippian jailer supposed to understand the word "saved" at all*? He could not read the minds of modern expositors. He had to depend on Paul and Silas for the clarification of this term.

Let us be reminded that the Greek word-group from which the terms "to save" and "salvation" are derived was one of the most fluid word-groups in the Greek language. Its range of possible referents was enormous. Even in the NT, the word "to save" (*sōzō*) is used in a variety of ways. If we take only the Gospel of Matthew, we find the verb ("to save") used of being "saved" from a storm (Matt 8:25), from drowning (Matt 14:30), from a disease (Matt 9:21-22), and from dying on the cross (Matt 27:40, 49).

No user of the Greek language could automatically assign a precise significance to this word without the aid of the speaker or the context.

The jailer was "about to kill himself." Although the prisoners were still there when Paul spoke to him, they might leave at any time. If they did, the jailer's own life would probably have been forfeit for allowing this to happen.

If all that Paul and Silas said to him were the words recorded in Acts 16:31, the jailer could well have concluded that by believing in this person named Jesus his physical life would be "saved." Maybe this "Lord" would somehow prevent the prisoners from escaping. In that case he would not die. That would have been a reasonable understanding of Paul's statement if the words in 16:31 stood alone.

But of course they did not stand alone. By the very nature of this narrative, we must assume that both the jailer and the evangelists meant these words in the sense that a Christian reader would understand them. This simply shows that either before or after Acts 16:31 was spoken, Paul and Silas gave the jailer the needed information.

In fact the text says so. Acts 16:32 reports, "And [Greek = *kai*] they spoke the word of the Lord to him and to all who were in his house." Paul preached the gospel in this man's house. What did Paul preach to that family? Luke has already told us in Acts 13:16-48.

The Sunday-school-class picture of the jailer being saved while Paul and Silas were still in the jail ignores Luke's text. According to Luke, before the jailer asked his question, "he brought them [Paul and Silas] out." Where did he take them? The answer suggested by Luke's story is that he took them to his own house (16:32) where he and his household heard "the word of the Lord" (16:32).

In this very condensed narrative, the following is the most likely scenario. The jailer brought Paul and Silas out of the prison and took them to his home. There Paul and Silas "spoke the word of the Lord" to the jailer and his family. The general content would have seen similar to Acts 13:23-37.

Upon hearing this exposition, the jailer speaks up and says, "Sirs, what must I do to be saved?" Paul and Silas give a reply that is heard not only by the jailer but also by his entire household (Acts 16:31), "'Believe on the Lord Jesus Christ, and you will be saved, *you and your household.*'"

What was the result of this evangelism? Luke records it in Acts 16:33-34:

> And he took them the same hour of the night and washed their stripes. And immediately he and all his family were baptized. Now when he had brought them into his house, he set food before them; and he rejoiced, having believed in God with *all his household* (emphasis added).

Following the sermon of Paul and Silas, the jailer graciously washes the wounds of the evangelists and the evangelists baptize him and his whole household. Then they eat together.

It was a joyful occasion for all. The jailer and his family rejoiced in their experience of salvation by faith. They were now *alive in Christ*! And we may be sure that the two evangelists rejoiced as well, for they had gathered "fruit for eternal life" (cf. John 4:36).

In Acts 16, Luke does not need to repeat the Pauline gospel found in Acts 13. He has already given that to us. Obviously Luke—and God's Spirit—expect the reader to pay attention.

CHAPTER 12

"Saved": The Last Word

It may surprise many that Acts 16:30-31 are the last references to eternal salvation until almost the end of the book (28:28). In the intervening chapters the only other uses of this word group ("to save"/"salvation") are found in Acts 27:20, 31, and 34. All three refer to being saved from death by shipwreck. Acts 16:31 stands as Luke's last statement of the truth that salvation is by faith in Jesus Christ.

The book of Acts is not about the doctrine of eternal salvation. Nevertheless it is important for Luke to show *what* Paul's doctrine was on that subject. This Luke does effectively through the narratives in Acts 13 and 16. There is no need for any further exposition of this truth in the rest of Luke's record.

It has often been said that Acts 16:31, along with John 3:16, are the two most fruitful salvation verses in the entire Bible. Probably more people can trace their salvation to one or the other of these verses than to any other verse or verses in God's Word.

Both verses refer to the same thing: namely, the giving of the gift of eternal life. No other definition for "saved" in Acts 16:31 has the slightest shred of Biblical evidence to support it. To be "saved" and to be "made alive" both mean the same thing for Paul (see again Eph 2:5 and the other texts cited above).

It is true that the divine blessings of "forgiveness" and "justification" occur at the same time that we are "made alive" in Christ. But Paul never uses either term as a functional equivalent for the "saved"/"salvation" concept. The reason is simple. Neither term expresses the basic, core idea of the word "saved" when that word is used of eternal salvation. For Paul, the fundamental sense of salvation is *always* to have, or to receive, eternal life. To be sure, "forgiveness" and "justification" are significant adjuncts of the salvation experience. But they are not its basic element.

God does not forgive spiritually dead people. He does not justify spiritually dead people. It is the born again person, *alive* in Christ, whom God forgives and justifies. Although new birth, forgiveness, and justification occur simultaneously at the moment of saving faith, the experience of regeneration is *logically prior* to the other two. It is to *a new man with a new life* that God grants the forgiveness of sins. It is to that same *new man* that he grants justification "from all things from which [he] could not be justified by the law of Moses" (Acts 13:39).

At the moment of salvation it is as though God said to the believer: *"You are now alive with the very life of My Son, and so all your sins are forgiven and you stand perfectly righteous in My sight."*

In fact, as Paul puts it in Rom 5:18, justification can be described as a "justification of life." As handled by the NASB, his words are: "even so through one act of righteousness there resulted justification of life to all men." But the translation of the Greek phrase here (*dikaiōsin zōēs*) could be better handled as "life's justification." Paul's phrase suggests that *life* is the true precursor of, and basis for, justification. (That he has *eternal* life in mind is shown by 5:21.)

The paraphrasing translation of the Jerusalem Bible (JB) is open to the objection that it implies universalism, but its handling of this phrase is helpful. The JB reads: "so the good act of one man brings everyone life and makes them justified." The bringing of life makes possible mankind's justification.

For this reason also, in Rom 1:17 Paul insists that "the one who is righteous by faith shall live" (as correctly understood by RSV, TEV, NIV, Barrett, Bruce, Byrne, Cranfield, Moo, and Nygren). Life is an inherent property of the justified believer. The justified believer does, and will, *live*.

Anyone who does not think that eternal life is fundamental to Paul's theology of salvation is not paying attention to either Paul or Luke.

CHAPTER 13

Jesus Said It First

We have stated that John 3:16 and Acts 16:31 mean the same thing. And indeed they do. In fact, this identification is established by John 3:17. In that verse we meet the *very first use* by Jesus of the word *saved* in the Fourth Gospel.

Let us read John 3:16 and 17 together:

> For God so loved the world that He gave His only begotten Son, that whoever believes in Him should not perish but have *everlasting life*. For God did not send His Son into the world to condemn the world, but that the world through Him might be *saved* (emphasis added).

It is transparent in these words of our Lord that the concepts of verse 17 parallel those of verse 16. The phrase *"should not perish"* (v 16) is paralleled by the words *"not...to condemn"* (v 17). Likewise, the phrase *"should have everlasting life"* (v 16) is paralleled by the words *"might be saved"* (v 17).

The equation of "saved" with "having eternal life" goes back to the Lord Jesus Christ Himself. *Jesus said it first!*

What else did we expect? Paul told us that his gospel "came through the revelation of Jesus Christ" (Gal 1:12). As far as Paul was concerned, this was the one and only gospel that God had given to men (see Gal 1:6-9). He preached what Jesus preached.

In yet another text where the words "saved" and "life" occur together (2 Tim 1:9-10), Paul tells us that:

> [God] has *saved* us and called us with a holy calling, not according to our works, but according to His own purpose

and grace which was given to us in Christ Jesus before time began, but has now been revealed by the appearing of our Savior Jesus Christ, who has abolished death and brought *life* and *immortality* to light through the gospel (emphasis added).

Above all else, when He preached to unsaved people, Jesus brought before them the truth of *life* and *immortality*. He brought these realities out into the light so that men could see them clearly. The Gospel of John as a whole shows Him doing exactly that. In fact, these very truths are superbly condensed by the famous words of John 11:25-26:

Jesus said to her [Martha], "I am the resurrection and the life. He who believes in me, though he may die, he shall live. And whoever lives and believes in Me, shall never die. Do you believe this?"

Clearly this is both physical *life* and *eternal/everlasting life* that are consummated forever in resurrection. There is no real death for the believer in Jesus. Though he can die physically, there is no end to the life Jesus bestows on him when he is saved. The believer is immortal!

Jesus made that clear. He brought these truths into the open. He did so, Paul informs us, *"through the gospel."*

So salvation for Paul *necessarily* meant unending life. Jesus said it first. And Paul preached it, because Jesus preached it. Do we?

Conclusion

Preachers of the gospel are profoundly responsible to God for what they preach. Humble, ordinary Christians are also responsible for what they tell unsaved people.

The offer God makes to us in the gospel is not something we can make up as we go along. Neither is it a kind of religious smorgasbord from which we may pick what we like and ignore the rest.

The gospel is not a postmodern concept marked by variety and diversity. The Biblical gospel is the message that Jesus preached and that the Apostle Paul preached. It is that and nothing else.

"Salvation" is not what *we* say it is. Salvation is what *Jesus* said it is. And "salvation" is what Paul said it is on the authority of Jesus Christ. To be "saved" is to be "made alive" with eternal life.

If we say to someone, "Believe on the Lord Jesus Christ and you will be saved," and we do not explain it the way Paul meant it, we are not being faithful to God's Word. And no Christian should be guilty of that kind of serious failure. People do not get saved because certain words are used, as if the words themselves were almost magical. It is God's *truth* that saves the believer.

As Peter puts it so well, "we have been born again, not of corruptible seed but incorruptible, through the word of God which lives and abides forever" (1 Pet 1:23). It is through God's incorruptible Word, not man's corruptible opinions, that we get eternal life. Therefore, in the proclamation of the gospel we can be nothing but mere conduits. We are simply channels for the saving message.

The source of that message is Jesus Christ our Lord.

Part III
Jesus: God's Prophet

CHAPTER 14

The Greatest Prophet

Jesus is coming again. He Himself said so. There could be no greater testimony to His return to earth than this.

In fact, the Lord Jesus Christ was the greatest prophet who ever walked on earth. There is no reason why He should not have been. He came to earth from the very bosom of the Father (John 1:18). He is the supreme Revealer (Heb 1:1-2).

Believers often recognize Jesus as a "Prophet, Priest, and King." And He *is* all these things. But of these three roles, the one we hear about the least is His office as a Prophet of God.

Despite the greatness of Jesus as a prophet, this aspect of His earthly ministry is often neglected. It is only vaguely appreciated (if appreciated at all) by many Christians. And yet in His prophetic teaching Jesus Christ gave us a brand-new perspective on His coming and on the end of the age.

This does not mean that Jesus gave us a "revision" of OT prophecy. On the contrary, He esteemed OT prophecy highly and often appealed to it. What it does mean is that Jesus gave us *fresh revelation*. He expanded on what had been disclosed through OT prophets.

In Acts 3:22-24, Peter was referring to Jesus when he said:

> For Moses truly said to the fathers, "The Lord your God will raise up for you a Prophet like me from your brethren. Him you shall hear in all things, whatever He says to you. And it shall be that every soul who will not hear that Prophet shall be utterly destroyed from among the people."

71

Moses was a rich source of *fresh* revelation. Among these were the creation story, the fall of man, the Tower of Babel, and the life of Abraham.

Although these accounts were most likely handed down by tradition, they could not be relied on as completely accurate. In the process of human transmission, they were easily garbled. The ancient pagan accounts of the flood story show this quite clearly. But Moses, the prophet, recorded them as they were divinely revealed to him. They were then perfect and reliable. The Mosaic Law was also revealed through him.

If Jesus was a prophet comparable to Moses, He must surely have revealed truth previously unknown or poorly understood among men.

It is not my purpose in this section to explore *everything* that was revealed by Jesus, God's Prophet. Instead, it is my intention to consider the revelation He gave about His own Second Coming to earth. The freshness—the newness—of this revelation is very impressive indeed.

To accomplish this goal we will look at Jesus' most famous prophetic discourse. It occurred on the Mount of Olives and has therefore been called the Olivet Discourse. It is reported in Matthew 24–25, Mark 13, and Luke 21. This section will consider this discourse as it is recorded in the Gospel of Matthew.

The Olivet Discourse is more than a prophetic discourse. It is *the* prophetic discourse. In fact, it is an indispensable bridge between OT and NT prophecy. Let's look at it carefully.

CHAPTER 15

The Coming of the Son of Man

In the Olivet Discourse, the Lord Jesus Christ taught something brand new about His own Second Coming.

Jesus on the Mount of Olives

On one occasion, Jesus was leaving the Jewish Temple. As He did so, He prophesied the Temple's utter destruction (Matt 24:1-2). He then proceeded to the Mount of Olives with His disciples. There they asked Him two questions that could only be answered by a prophet (v 3).

Jesus' response to these questions is recorded in Matt 24:4–25:46. It is the longest uninterrupted prophetic discussion found anywhere in the NT outside the book of Revelation.

It is also Christianity's most important prophetic presentation. Without it we could hardly understand the other prophetic passages in the NT, *including* the book of Revelation. The Olivet Discourse is indispensable for us. It is the key to understanding the end times as they are presented in the NT Scriptures.

The Mount of Olives was a most appropriate setting for our Lord's prophetic teaching. At the battle of Armageddon, Zech 14:3-4 tells us that "the Lord will go forth and fight against those nations, as He fights in the day of battle. And in that day His feet will stand on *the Mount of Olives*, which faces Jerusalem on the east" (emphasis added). As NT people know, "the Lord" in Zech 14:3 is Jesus Christ Himself.

Our Lord's great prophetic discourse took place on the very mountain where His feet will stand again when He delivers Jerusalem from its enemies. Not surprisingly, the theme of the Olivet Discourse is His own Second Coming (or, Second Advent).

The key word for "coming" in this discourse is the Greek word *parousia*. It occurs four times in the discourse (Matt 24:3, 27, 37, 39). It is found nowhere else in the Gospel of Matthew. It is one way that Matthew emphasizes that the Olivet Discourse is *the* discourse about our Savior's return to earth.

Of course, there is no doubt that the Second Advent is a major subject of OT prophecy. But in this discussion by our Lord, we learn truth about His future return that we could not have learned from the OT alone.

The Arrival of the Second Advent

After hearing Jesus predict the destruction of the Temple, the disciples raised two questions.

Their questions were recorded in Matt 24:3:

(1) "Tell us, when will these things be?"

(2) "And what will be the sign of Your coming
    and of the end of the age?".

Jesus does not get to the first question until the discourse reaches Matt 24:36. But for our purposes, we will consider question one first.

Taking the two questions together, we see that the disciples were thinking in terms of the end times. The words "coming" and "end of the age" make this quite clear. Obviously, they connected the prophecy about the destruction of the Temple with the end times as well. But their words in question number one do not refer to *that event alone*. Instead, the phrase *"these things"* is very broad. It is precisely this term that Jesus picks up in Matt 24:33-34.

As recorded in Matthew, the Olivet Discourse does not contain anything about when the Temple would be destroyed. But Jesus *did* address that issue in this discourse as we learn from Luke 21:12-24. Those verses in Luke are not found in Matthew. They cover events (in 66-70 AD) that are specifically said to take place *before* the end time events mentioned in Luke 21:10-11. But *how long* before is not stated.

The destruction of the Temple *could have been* part of the end times, because the kingdom of God is re-offered to Israel in Acts (see Acts 1:6-7; 3:19-26). But Matthew only reports what Jesus said about the *actual events* of the end times. The timing of these future events is addressed in Matt 24:36-42.

"Tell us when...?" the disciples ask. So to speak, Jesus replies, "No I won't." His actual words are, "But of that day and hour no one knows, not even the angels of heaven, but My Father only" (Matthew 24:36).

This statement is also recorded in Mark 13:32. There the phrase "nor the Son" is included. These additional words in Mark show us that the answer to the question about "when" was not present in Jesus' human consciousness. Of course, as God He was omniscient. However, as inadequate as it is to say it this way, Jesus had "blocked" this fact from His human mind.

Matthew 24:36 focuses on a very important point. As we shall see shortly, the question about "when" pertains to Christ's Second Advent. The "when" of the Second Advent is unknowable to man. It is also unknowable in the angelic sphere. This knowledge properly belongs to God the Father. Since the Son only reveals what the Father wants to reveal, Jesus, God's Prophet, leaves that knowledge in His Father's hands.

This significant truth leads directly to *new revelation*. Jesus immediately goes on to say,

> But as the days of Noah were, *so also will the coming of the Son of Man be*. For as in the days before the flood, they were eating and drinking, marrying and giving in marriage, until the day that Noah entered the ark, and did not know until the flood came and took them all away, *so also will the coming of the Son of Man be* (Matt 24:37-39, emphasis added).

Here we learn something never disclosed in OT prophecy. It is this: that "*the coming of the Son of man*" will be as totally unexpected as the flood that came suddenly in Noah's day. In fact, until the arrival of the flood, normal human activity went on as it always had. That is to say, human beings ate and drank, married and gave in marriage. Mankind had no clue ("they knew not") that they were about to be swept away in a worldwide disaster. The same thing, Jesus says (twice), will be true of *"the coming of the Son of Man."*

Obviously, if the Father alone knows the time of this event, no angel or human being can possibly give mankind a warning that it is about to happen. The surprise is totally guaranteed.

The Worldwide Disaster

But something else is also obvious from our Lord's words in vv 37-39. The Second Coming brings with it an *unexpected* worldwide disaster. It will be like the flood, Jesus says, that "took them all away" (Matt 24:39).

Earlier in this passage, the disciples heard Jesus discuss another time of trouble. In the opening section of the Olivet Discourse (24:4-14), Jesus had described a world filled with problems. Life on earth will be disrupted by nation rising against nation, kingdom against kingdom, and by "famines, pestilences, and earthquakes in various places" (vv 6-7). In v 8, Jesus calls these events "the beginning of labor pains" (NKJV = "the beginning of sorrows").

The Greek word here for "labor pains," or "sorrows," is *odin* [*ohden*]. It refers to the childbearing pains of a woman who has begun the process of giving birth. In Biblical prophecy, it is a term that describes the eschatological—or final—calamities of the present age (for example, 1 Thess 5:2-3, discussed below).

The events Jesus describes are agonies that can be compared to birth pains. A new age in human history is being born. The Kingdom of God will be visibly present on earth. The world will have a period of anguish until the birth of that wonderful age is fully realized.

But the labor pains that are mentioned in vv 6-8 are only the "beginning." They will be followed by more severe worldwide agonies. In the following section of the discourse (Matt 24:15-31), Jesus makes this plain. The calamities of the end times will reach an intensity that is without parallel in human history. The preliminary labor pains are intense enough to show that God's judgments have begun. Yet they are only the start.

In describing the full intensity of the final troubles, Jesus states:

> For then there will be great tribulation, such as has not
> been since the beginning of the world until this time, no,

nor ever shall be. And unless those days were shortened, no flesh would be saved; but for the elect's sake those days will be shortened (vv 21-22).

In these words Jesus is referring to what is often called "the Great Tribulation." But the English word *tribulation* hides an important connection that a Greek hearer or reader could make. The word *tribulation* translates the Greek word *thlipsis*. That word, too, may be used to describe the anguish of childbirth. It is actually used that way by Jesus Himself in John 16:21. There Jesus says:

> A woman, when she is in labor, has sorrow because her hour has come; but as soon as she has given birth to the child, she no longer remembers the anguish [*thlipsis*] for joy that a human being has been born into the world.

Therefore, Jesus' two phrases, the "Great Tribulation" and the "beginning of labor pains," are clearly connected. The "Great Tribulation" might also be called the "Great Travail." The initial, intermittent birth pains of a pregnant woman signal the onset of the more prolonged, definitive *travail* pains of the actual birth. The judgments of the end times will be like that. Jesus' teaching about the "beginning of labor pains" and the "Great Travail" are two parts of the same truth. The end times contain the *birth pains* of the new age.

This whole period of time is the subject of Matt 24:4-31. Once the Great Travail is over, the world seems to be coming to an end (note 24:29). But instead, "the *sign of the Son of Man* will appear in heaven, and then all the tribes of the earth will mourn, and they will see the Son of Man coming on the clouds of heaven with power and great glory" (24:30, emphasis added).

Then, too, the "elect," that is, born-again people here on earth, will be gathered into His presence (Matt 24:31; see 24:22, 24). Their numbers will be great. This is because a worldwide evangelization has taken place during these troubled times (Matt 24:14; see Rev 7:9, 13-14). Somewhat later *all* living Gentiles will be brought before the King (Matt 25:31-32).

With the use of the word *sign* in 24:30—for the first time since the disciples used it in 24:3—Jesus indicates the conclusion of His answer to their *second* question. Their second question was, "And what will be *the sign* of your coming, and of the end of the age?"

(24:3). The Son of Man Himself, evidently, is the *sign*. His glorious appearing heralds the end of this present age.

The appearance of Jesus to all mankind follows the period of labor pains (Matt 24:29a). Out of horrendous turmoil and trouble, a new age will be *born*. As with the birth of a child (John 16:21), this new age will produce an overflowing supply of joy (see Rev 19:6-7).

Anticipating the End of the Age

Following His powerful description of the conclusion of our age, Jesus presents a brief exhortation (24:32-35). This exhortation is based on a parable about a budding fig tree. Jesus' point is made clear when He applies the parable, "So you also, when you see *all these things*, know that it is near, at the very doors" (Matt 24:33, emphasis added).

The disciples living at that time are to recognize the nearness of "the end of the age" by observing *all these things* (note "these things" in 24:3). As they watch the events Jesus has prophesied run their course—as they see *all these things* taking place—they will know that the "summer" of the age to come "is near" (see v 32). Furthermore, the generation that sees these events *begin* will also see them *end*.

This is stated in Matt 24:34: "Assuredly, I say to you, *this generation* will by no means pass away till *all these things* take place" (emphasis added). Of course, Jesus could not be talking here about the generation alive at the time He spoke. As is often true in prophecy, the standpoint of the prophet is in the time period of the events that are foreseen. Jesus is standing prophetically in *the very generation* that will experience these things. It is *this* generation that will not pass away until everything He has foretold takes place.

To be sure, the disasters of this period will stir up the world's anxiety as never before. But believers living at that time can rest assured that the calamities are not going to go on without end. Instead, they will be completed within the life span of a single generation. In fact, the glorious conclusion of these troubles is guaranteed by the words of Jesus Himself. He says, "Heaven and earth will pass away, but My words will by no means pass away" (24:35).

If the disciples have been paying attention, they will already have learned a great deal from the Olivet Discourse. Although Jesus refers once to Daniel the prophet (24:15), by and large His treatment of this period of time has no real precedent in OT prophecy, although the OT prophets knew about the coming of the final calamities. But none of them gives us anywhere near as detailed a description of this period of time as Jesus does here.

There is one issue Jesus must still discuss. It is the issue of *when*. *When* will this unprecedented series of events begin to run its course? When, in fact, will *all these things* take place (v 34)?

As we have already seen, there is no specific answer to this question. The reason is that *"of that day and hour no one knows…but My Father only"* (v 36).

Clarifying the Second Coming

Up to this point in our Lord's Discourse, the disciples may have thought that Jesus' coming occurred at precisely the same time as the end of the age. The Greek form of their second question (24:3) implies that these two things are very closely related, which of course they are. But Jesus now goes on to show them that these events are not simultaneous at all.

As we saw above, Jesus flatly declares that His coming (*parousia*) is as sudden and unexpected as the flood was in Noah's day. The flood came at a time when nothing out of the ordinary had taken place. But this would not be true of His coming if His coming occurs *at the conclusion* of the Great Tribulation. This obvious problem is often ignored. Many readers have thought that Matt 24:29-30 places the coming *there*. But this is a mistake.

Matthew 24:29-31 definitely does not use Jesus' special word for coming (that is, the word *parousia*). The passage *does* say that the tribulation is immediately followed by unparalleled heavenly events involving the sun, moon, and stars. These heavenly events are followed in turn by *the sign* of the Son of Man. But the word *parousia* is not used.

This sign is not specified precisely, but the Greek can be read as meaning "the sign that *is* the Son of Man." If taken in this way, the sign refers to His appearance in glory. That, after all, is stated in the following words: "they will see the Son of Man coming [Greek = *erchomenon*] on the clouds of heaven" (v 30).

But to see Him "coming" like this is not the same as describing His descent from the presence of God. In fact, it *can't be* precisely that. At the time that men see Him this way He is *already* on the clouds that are found in earth's atmosphere. But when did His coming from God's presence begin? When, in fact, did the *parousia* really start?

The answer is plain. The coming (*parousia*) begins at the time when God's judgments begin, for "the coming of the Son of Man" will be like the coming of the flood in Noah's day (24:37-39). Therefore, it will occur at a time when uninterrupted human life is continuing as usual, just as it was before the flood.

This means that "the coming of the Son of Man" cannot *begin* at the time described in 24:29-31. *That time* is "immediately after the tribulation of those days." And the tribulation is a period of such severe trouble that "unless those days were shortened, no flesh would be saved" (24:22).

To put this another way, "the coming [*parousia*] of the Son of Man" starts *without a sign*. It is only *after* "the tribulation of those days" that "the *sign* of the Son of Man will appear in heaven" (24:30, emphasis added). This conclusion leads to another. The term for coming (*parousia*) does not simply refer to an *arrival*. It clearly covers a *span of time*.

This agrees perfectly with the general use of the word *parousia* in Greek. In fact, this is indicated in the standard Greek-English Lexicon of the NT (BDAG). There the first type of meaning given is, "the state of being present at a place," or more simply, "presence" (p. 780). The second type of meaning given is that of an "arrival as the first stage in presence," or more simply, "coming."

As it happens, English has a word that is roughly similar, namely the word *advent*. When we speak of the First Advent or the Second Advent of our Lord, the words suggest not merely His *arrival* but also His subsequent *presence* in the world.

We may say that the Second Advent *begins* unexpectedly when the judgments of God begin. However, it is *disclosed* by "the sign of the Son of Man"—namely, by our Lord's appearance in "the clouds of heaven" when the Great Tribulation is over.

Precision in Prophecy

Someone may object that I am being too precise in interpreting our Lord's words. But the Scriptures teach us to interpret with this level of precision. In fact, a lack of precision in interpreting His words often results in serious errors. This is clearly illustrated in a passage found in John 21:20-23.

According to John 21, our Lord predicted the death of Peter (John 21:18-19). Peter then turned to look at the beloved disciple (John) and asked, "But Lord, what about this man?" Jesus replied, "If I will that he remain till I come, what is that to you?" (21:21-22). The Apostle John then adds some significant words:

> Then the saying went out among the brethren that this dis-
> ciple would not die. Yet Jesus did not say to him that he
> would not die, but "If I will that he remain till I come, what
> is that to you?" (John 21:23).

Jesus' words were misunderstood because insufficient atten-
tion was paid to the little word "if"! Close attention to our Lord's words, therefore, is essential in order to avoid rushing to improper conclusions.

Students of Matthew's Gospel should pay close attention to *exactly* what Jesus said in Matt 24:36-39. If they do, they will never think that His coming (*parousia*) begins only *after* an unprecedented period of earthly trouble. That view is impossible in Matt 24:36-39. And this impossibility is due to a new feature of Biblical prophecy that Jesus reveals. This feature is the totally unexpected arrival of Jesus from heaven while life on earth goes on as before.

This is a new revelation by God's greatest Prophet.

But even if we misunderstand it, the apostles did not. It is Peter, for example, who writes about scoffers who will say, "Where is the promise of His coming (*parousia*)? For since the fathers fell asleep, all things continue as they were from the beginning of creation" (2 Pet 3:4). *Things go on as always*, they insist, *and the parousia hasn't occurred!*

Strikingly, Peter attributes the ignorance of these scoffers to will-
ful forgetfulness of the *flood* (2 Pet 3:5-6). A few verses later he states that "the day of the Lord will come *as a thief in the night*" — that is, without warning (2 Pet 3:10, emphasis added). The sudden-
ness of the *parousia*, and the comparison with the flood, are ideas Peter got directly from our Lord. Jesus taught them in the Olivet Discourse.

In the same way, the Apostle Paul also reflects this teaching. In describing the coming of the Day of the Lord he writes, "For you yourselves know perfectly that the day of the Lord so comes *as a thief in the night*. For when they say, 'Peace and safety!' then sudden destruction comes upon them, *as labor pains upon a pregnant woman*. And they shall not escape" (1 Thess 5:2-3, emphasis added). The prophetic teaching of our Lord appears here quite clearly, including a reference to "labor pains."

After urging the Thessalonians to be watchful and not allow the Day of the Lord to overtake them as a thief (1 Thess 5:4-8), Paul adds these words:

> For God did not appoint us to wrath, but to obtain salvation [= deliverance] through our Lord Jesus Christ, who died for us, that whether we wake or sleep we should *live together with Him* (1 Thess 5:9-10, emphasis added).

This important statement elaborates an earlier one by Paul. The Thessalonians, he said, were waiting for God's "Son from heaven… who *delivers* us from the wrath to come" (1 Thess 1:10, emphasis added).

Unmistakably, therefore, both Paul and Peter link together several things. These are:

(1) the Day of the Lord,
(2) the Second Advent, and
(3) an earthly situation in which there is
      no expectation of calamity.

Men are saying "peace and safety," and they are insisting that "all things continue as they were from the beginning of creation." The Day of the Lord will come unexpectedly like *a thief in the night*. All of this, as we have just seen, is firmly rooted in a careful reading of the Olivet Discourse.

To repeat: The beginning of the Second Advent has no *sign*. It suddenly overtakes an unsuspecting world that falsely thinks that all is well. Careful attention to *precisely* what Jesus said on the Mount of Olives compels this understanding.

One Shall Be Taken

Paul's words in 1 Thessalonians (quoted above) also focus on something else. They focus on the theme of *deliverance* from the calamities of the Day of the Lord.

In fact, Paul saw the Second Coming as the way God's Son *delivers us from the wrath to come* (1:10). Although "sudden destruction" (5:3) will overtake the world "as a thief in the night" (5:2), the Day of the Lord need not catch believers by surprise. *They* will be delivered.

Therefore Paul states, "But you, brethren, are not in darkness, so that this Day should overtake you as a thief" (5:4). Instead, "You are all sons of light and sons of the day. We are not of the night nor of darkness. Therefore let us not sleep, as others do, but let us watch and be sober" (5:5-6). *Stay awake*, Paul says. *Don't be caught by surprise like the world around you.*

Moreover Paul urges them to put on "as a helmet the hope of salvation [deliverance]" (5:8). Why? Because "God did not appoint us to wrath [that is, to the wrath of the Day of the Lord (5:2-3)], but to obtain salvation [deliverance] through our Lord Jesus Christ" so that *"we should live together with Him"* (5:9-10; emphasis added). Our destiny, says Paul, is not the coming wrath but living in the presence of Christ.

Where did Paul get this idea? Can it be found in our Lord's Olivet Discourse? The answer is yes, it can.

Immediately after describing His coming (*parousia*) as an unexpected event, Jesus adds these familiar words,

> Then two men will be in the field: one will be taken and the other left. Two women will be grinding at the mill: one will be taken and the other left (Matt 24:40-41).

We should notice first of all the word *then*. Its immediate reference is back to the preceding phrase about "the coming of the Son of Man." The *then* refers to something that happens at the time when His coming begins.

Of particular interest also is the word Jesus chooses for *taken*. The Greek word *paralambanō* is used here in its main NT sense. The word's first meaning as defined by the standard dictionary (BDAG, p. 767) is: "to take into close association, *take (to oneself), take with/along*." Other examples in Matthew can be found in 1:20-21 (Joseph "taking" Mary as his wife), 2:13, 14, 20, 21 (Joseph "taking" the child Jesus to Egypt and back to Israel), and 17:1 (Jesus "taking along" the three disciples to the mount of transfiguration). There are additional examples in Matthew, but these can serve as illustrations of the word's primary use.

Therefore, the word *paralambanō* (vv 40-41) is a quite different word than the one in the statement "the flood came and *took* them all *away*" (v 39). The word rendered "take away" in v 39 is *airō*. In v 39 the Lord is speaking about being swept away in judgment. But *paralambanō* in vv 40-41 does not suggest that idea in any way. In fact, the shift to a verb with a different meaning suggests just the opposite.

As I have noted, Matt 24:40-41 follows our Lord's statement that "so also will the coming of the Son of Man be" (v 39). Immediately after saying this, He declares that *then* some will be selectively "*taken along*." Specifically, one of two men "in the field" will be *taken along*, and one of two women "grinding at the mill." This can hardly mean anything else but that such people are "taken along" *with His coming*. That is to say, He comes and *takes them along with Him*.

Very simply and plainly, Jesus is saying that, when He comes, He will "take along with Him" certain individuals that are on earth at that time. Paul fills in the details of this when he writes:

> For the Lord Himself will descend from heaven with a shout, with the voice of an archangel, and with the trumpet of God. And the dead in Christ will rise first. Then we who are alive and remain shall be caught up together with them in the clouds to meet the Lord in the air. And then we shall always be *with the Lord* (1 Thess 4:16-17, emphasis added).

In other words, when Jesus descends from heaven, He will *take along with Himself* all the believers on earth. He will do this by catching them up into the clouds to meet Him. They will be *with Him* from then on. To put it another way, after this event they will "live together with Him" (1 Thess 5:10). The removal of believers from the earth is often referred to by a traditional term: the Rapture.

Therefore, the coming of God's Son will *deliver us from the wrath to come* (1 Thess 1:9). It will deliver us from all the calamities that will overtake the unsaved world. This truth has its roots in the Olivet Discourse.

CHAPTER 16

Living in the Light of His Coming

After revealing that the second advent will arrive unexpectedly (Matt 24:36-41), the Lord Jesus Christ begins a new section of His discourse. In this section, He teaches His disciples how to live in the light of His coming. The new section extends all the way from Matt 24:42–25:46. The first unit of this material is found in Matt 24:42–25:13.

Matthew 24:42 begins with the words, "Watch therefore, for you do not know what hour your Lord is coming." It concludes with similar words in Matt 25:13, "Watch therefore, for you know neither the day nor the hour in which the Son of Man is coming." In both these verses, the word "watch" is a Greek verb (*gregoreō*) that basically means "to stay awake," "to be alert."

The literary technique called *inclusio* is one where the end of a section contains an idea or words that are similar to an idea or words at the beginning of the section. Matt 25:13 forms an *inclusio* for the unit beginning in 24:42. This *inclusio* indicates that Matt 24:42–25:13 is a distinct sub-unit in the Olivet Discourse. Let's consider this important body of material.

Staying Awake for the Thief

If the "coming of the Son of Man" is to be as unexpected as the coming of the flood, then those who belong to Christ should stay alert. Following an exhortation to stay awake (v 42), verse 43 introduces the theme of the "thief." Jesus speaks these words:

> But know this, that if the master of the house had known
> what hour the thief would come, he would have watched
> [*stayed awake*] and not allowed his house to be broken into.

Very clearly we have here the source for a concept expressed by
Peter and Paul. According to both of them, the Day of the Lord
[that is, our Lord's Second Advent] will come like "a thief in the
night." Peter and Paul were good students of God's Prophet.

Jesus' analogy about the coming of a thief has implications for
His disciples. The householder ("master of the house") needed to
stay awake for the obvious reason that only by doing so could he
be ready for the thief. He needed to be *ready* to prevent the thief
from breaking into his house and stealing from him. In our Lord's
words, if the homeowner had been alert he would "*not have allowed
his house to be broken into*" (24:43).

This parable about the thief is followed by an admonition to be
ready. After having told His disciples to stay awake (v 42), Jesus now
adds:

> Therefore you also be *ready*, for the Son of Man is coming
> at an hour you do not expect (Matt 24:44, emphasis added).

By comparing His own coming to that of a "thief," Jesus teaches
His disciples a basic fact. If someone is not *ready* for a "thief" he
will suffer loss. In other words, the thief will "take" something
away. This implies that the unprepared servant of Christ will lose
something of value when His Lord returns.

To drive this point home, Jesus proceeds to tell two parables
that underscore it. The first parable is about a servant whose *conduct* leaves him unready for his Lord's return (Matt 24:45-51). The
second is about five women whose *neglect* leaves them unready as
well (Matt 25:1-12). Both the servant and the five women suffer
significant losses. In a sense, both stories teach the same lesson—
being unprepared leads to serious loss.

Let us now look at each of these stories.

The Unprepared Servant: Matthew 24:45-51

The opening words about an unprepared servant are an exhortation to avoid the trap into which he fell. Jesus begins by saying,

> Who then is a faithful and wise servant, whom his master made ruler over his household, to give them food in due season? Blessed is that servant whom his master, when he comes, will find so doing. Assuredly, I say to you that he will make him ruler over all his goods (Matt 24:45-47).

"Which of you," Jesus is saying, "wants to be a reliable servant like this? Such a servant will be blessed when His Lord comes and finds him properly engaged in his assigned activities. In fact, that servant will be promoted to a more responsible position with greater authority." Certainly this brief exhortation should inspire every believer in Christ to keep busy serving the Lord.

But there is an alternative. The servant "whom his master made ruler over his household" (v 45) may turn out *not* to be "faithful and wise." Jesus describes this possibility as He continues His parable:

> But if that evil servant says in his heart, "My master is delaying his coming," and begins to beat his fellow servants, and to eat and drink with the drunkards, the master of that servant will come on a day when he is not looking for him and at an hour he is not aware of (Matt 24:48-50).

What causes the downfall of this evil servant? Very simply put, he stops *watching* for his master.

In his heart the servant says, "My master is delaying his coming." And if his master is not going to come anytime soon, this servant is not concerned when his own faithfulness begins to deteriorate. As a result he "begins" (v 49) to mistreat his master's other servants—those he was assigned to feed, not to beat! He also begins to behave personally in a self-indulgent and undisciplined manner.

Suddenly his master comes as unexpectedly as a thief in the night. The end result for this servant is sobering. Jesus says:

> …the master of that servant…will cut him in two and appoint him his portion with the hypocrites. There shall be weeping and gnashing of teeth (Matt 24:50-51).

The master's judgment "cuts him in two"—a metaphor, undoubtedly, since he can still be assigned "his portion with the hypocrites." That is to say, he is assigned to the ignominy and loss that properly belong to hypocrites. His hypocrisy was evident. While occupying a position of service to his master, he had actually served himself to the detriment of others. He will therefore deeply regret his failure and will express his remorse with "weeping and gnashing of teeth" (v 51).

Some readers might think that this servant's fate, as described by Jesus, means that he is going to hell. However, the language does not require such an interpretation. The implication that a sword is used in the servant's judgment reminds us that the word of God will be the instrument of our Lord's judgment of believers.

In Heb 4:12-13 we are told that "the word of God is living and powerful, and sharper than any two-edged sword, piercing even to the division of soul and spirit." In addition, His word is "a discerner of the thoughts and intents of the heart," since "all things are naked and open to the eyes of Him *to whom we must give an account*" (emphasis added).

No doubt when our Lord judges unfaithful servants by His penetrating *word*, such servants will feel as if they have been "cut apart." Rebuke by Christ at His Judgment Seat (often called, the *Bema*) will certainly be a spiritually painful experience.

The words about "weeping and gnashing of teeth" do not really suggest hell either. In the culture of the ancient Middle East such anguished displays of grief were well understood as appropriate to deep sorrow and loss. And although this first parable does not stress the fact, this unfaithful servant *has* suffered loss. He has *lost* the *promotion* to greater authority (see v 47) that would have been his had he remained "faithful and wise." Instead he suffered *demotion*. In this life he had ruled (v 45). After His Lord's return, he will not (see 2 Tim 2:12).

Instead of being faithful and wise, he had stopped expecting that his master might come at any time. On the contrary, he had decided that, "My master is delaying his coming." The result was that his *conduct* deteriorated seriously. He was not ready for His master's arrival and assessment. He is therefore judged severely and is denied elevation to a new level of service.

The Unprepared Women: Matthew 25:1-13

The second parable involves women who are also unprepared to meet their coming lord (Matt 25:1-13). In this parable, however, there is no misconduct on their part as there was with the unfaithful servant. Instead we find five women, out of a total of ten, who are unprepared because of their *neglect*. They have not made the necessary preparations. They are not *ready* for Him to arrive.

This parable complements the previous one as a servant of Christ can be unprepared for His Lord's coming either through serious *misconduct* or through simple *neglect*.

This second parable revolves around ten women who are waiting for a bridegroom to come. The opening verse (Matt 25:1) is best understood as a summary of the story that follows. In the story, ten virgin women are at the scene of the coming wedding feast. They are waiting for the arrival of the bridegroom and his party.

All ten of the women have torches with them—"torches" is a better word here than "lamps" (NKJV). In a helpful article entitled, "Lampades in Matthew 25:1-13," (in *Soli Deo Gloria* [John Knox Press, 1968], pp. 83-87), Joachim Jeremias has pointed out that the role of these women at the banquet was most likely that of entertainers. Their task was to perform the torch dance once the celebration began. To be allowed to display their skills on such an occasion was a privilege they clearly valued.

While they wait for the bridegroom, all ten of the virgins catch up on their sleep. By doing so, they will be fresh and ready to perform their role when the time arrives (v 5). There is nothing wrong with this. That is clear from the fact that the wise virgins sleep as well as the foolish ones.

When the cry comes at midnight that the bridegroom is approaching, all ten of the virgins wake up. At once they begin to light their torches (vv 6-7). If, as seems likely, these torches burned oil-soaked rags, oil had to be poured on them frequently to keep them burning. The foolish virgins realize they have *neglected* to bring containers holding extra oil. They will need this oil if their torches are to stay lighted for the celebration.

In vain the foolish virgins ask to borrow oil from their wiser companions. But their request is denied (vv 8-9). The wise virgins know that they may need all the oil they have. So they advise their foolish companions to go off to the merchants and buy their own oil (v 9). Since it is already midnight (see v 6) it may be hard to find merchants willing to sell to them at that hour of the night. The business day is long over.

Eventually the necessary oil is obtained. But by the time the five foolish virgins return to the house, the bridegroom has already arrived and gone inside, accompanied by the five wise virgins (vv 10-11). The five women knock vigorously at the door requesting to be admitted (v 11). They shout, "Lord, Lord, open to us" (v 11). From within, their Lord denies them admission with the words, "Assuredly, I say to you, I do not know you."

Again the parabolic nature of this story must be kept in mind. We are not to pour unwarranted theology into it. The five foolish virgins are not sent away to some horrible form of torment. In the parable, the words "I do not know you" are a way of denying their request to get inside. The celebration will go on without them. They will not be allowed to perform their torch dance.

Unquestionably, these foolish virgins represent believers. They believe that the bridegroom is coming and are eager to play their role when he comes. Their problem is *not* unbelief, but a failure to be prepared that is rooted in *neglect*. "Those who were foolish... took no oil with them" (v 3).

The Scriptures give us many instructions for preparing to meet our Lord. The simplest summary of these is found in the words of the Apostle John, who wrote:

> And now, little children, *abide in Him*, that when He appears, we may have confidence and not be ashamed before Him at His coming [*parousia*] (1 John 2:28, emphasis added).

When we *abide in Christ*, the Holy Spirit keeps the flame of spiritual warmth and vitality burning in our hearts and lives. But the Spirit's work in us comes at the "cost" of time, energy, and dedication to God and His word. However, if we are willing to pay that price, the Biblical writers will "sell" us their extremely valuable "oil," God's truth. In that way we can keep our lives burning brightly for Him until He returns.

The wise virgins bought their oil ahead of time. As the foolish virgins found out, you can't get the needed oil in a hurry after a long period of neglect. If we *neglect* spiritual readiness, we will suffer loss when our Lord comes back.

Suffering Loss

A thief brings loss to those whom he robs. In both of our Lord's parables, loss is experienced when the master or bridegroom comes.

In the parable about the unfaithful servant, the servant *loses* a significant promotion. His master caught him by surprise. He came "on a day when he [was] not looking for him and at an hour that he [was] not aware of" (Matt 24:50).

In the case of the foolish virgins, they *lose* the opportunity to perform their role (the torch dance) at the wedding celebration. In their case, although they are wide awake at the proper time along with the wise virgins, the foolish virgins are *inadequately prepared*.

So Jesus concludes this unit by saying,

> "Watch [= *stay alert*] therefore, for you know neither the day nor the hour in which the Son of Man is coming" (Matt 25:13).

As mentioned earlier, this verse forms an *inclusio* with 24:42. That verse, like 25:13, exhorts believers to watch. They are to stay awake and alert. But in 25:13 we also meet the combination of "day" and "hour" for the first time since 24:36. These two verses should also be compared:

> "But of that *day and hour* no one knows…" (Matt 24:36, emphasis added).

> "…for you know neither *the day nor the hour* in which the Son of Man is coming" (Matt 25:13, emphasis added).

Here we have a double *inclusio*. Matthew 25:13 does conclude the material about the servant and the ten virgins (24:42—25:13). But it also concludes the whole discussion about *the complete uncertainty* of "the day and the hour" when the Son of Man's coming will begin (24:36—25:13).

In both parables, Jesus is teaching us that staying spiritually alert for His coming will prevent significant personal loss. And in turn, alertness involves watching our conduct and not neglecting proper spiritual preparations.

This is brand new prophetic truth. It is truth that was taught for the first time in Biblical history by Jesus of Nazareth in His role as God's Prophet.

Since we live in the days *before* His coming (*parousia*) the truth of Matt 24:36–25:13 is all intended for *our* learning and *our* admonition. The message is clear. We should always be ready (24:44) for Him. If we are not ready, we will suffer significant *loss* at the Judgment Seat of Christ (1 Cor 3:10-15; 2 Cor 5:10).

CHAPTER 17

The Prophecy and the People of God

The truth that Jesus taught in His discourse on the Mount of Olives is important for another reason. This is because it reveals a basic distinction that the later NT writers build on extensively.

We live in a democratic society where people assume that our government should treat all its citizens in the same way, regardless of race, gender, or religion. But God is not required to govern by democratic principles. He is fair and He is not a respecter of persons (Rom 2:11), but this does not mean that every individual, group, or nation has exactly the same relationship to Him as every other.

God's way of dealing with human beings is not dully monochrome, but is a highly variegated, multicolored picture. A thoughtful reading of 1 Corinthians 12 illustrates this clearly at the level of spiritual functions. The spiritual Body of Christ is a unity with rich variety.

The principle of *variety* also exists at the level of large groups of people. Let's look at the Olivet Discourse again with this in mind.

The People Who Live During the Second Advent

Our Lord's teaching about His Second Coming points clearly to two different groups of people. On the one hand, there are those who are "taken along with Him" when His coming begins (Matt 24:40-41). These people will no longer be on earth once the judgments of the Second Advent have begun. On the other hand, there are those who will be on earth during the events of the Great Tribulation.

Let us consider this second group first, just as Jesus does in His discourse.

Of particular interest are the warnings Jesus gives to those who will live in this future time. As we have seen, it is a time marked out by two related terms. The first of these is the phrase "the beginning of labor pains" (Matt 24:8). The second is the "Great Travail" (= the "Great Tribulation," 24:21).

During what Jesus describes as "the beginning of labor pains," He counsels His followers by saying, "See that you are not troubled; for all these things must come to pass, but the end is not yet" (Matt 24:6b).

During this initial time period His followers are not to become "troubled." The first disturbances (24:5-6a, 7-8) do not herald the nearness of "the end." By "the end" our Lord is obviously referring to what His disciples had called "the end of the age" (Matt 24:3).

However, after His reference to "the beginning of labor pains" (Matt 24:8), Jesus describes a period of persecution for His followers. This will also be a period of worldwide evangelization (24:9-14).

His last statement in these verses makes this clear:

> "And this gospel of the kingdom will be preached in all the world as a witness to all the nations, and *then the end will come*" (Matt 24:14, emphasis added).

Let us carefully note the word "then" with which 24:9 begins ("*then* they will deliver you up..."). With this word Jesus signals that when "the beginning of labor pains" has taken place (v 8), the period during which His followers are not to be "troubled" will be over.

The following period ("then") will bring them trouble. It will also bring the privilege of evangelizing the nations (24:9-14). His disciples will do this even though they "will be hated by all nations for [His] name's sake" (v 9). But once this task is completed, *then the end will come* (24:14).

Clearly a new time period is under consideration in Matt 24:9-14. Yet how will the disciples of Jesus in that day know that this period has begun? The answer is given in Matt 24:15ff.

Jesus' words there are famous. The first word (in English) is the word "therefore" (in Greek this word is the second one in the verse). In the light of the coming period of persecution and evangelization, Jesus is saying, *therefore* do as follows.

His instructions are based on an OT prophecy from the Book of Daniel. But the instructions themselves are brand new. Once again God's Prophet is speaking newly revealed truth:

> Therefore when you see the *'abomination of desolation,'* spoken of by Daniel the prophet, standing in the holy place (whoever reads, let him understand), then let those who are in Judea flee to the mountains. Let him who is on the house-top not go down to take anything out of his house. And let him who is in the field not go back to get his clothes. But woe to those who are pregnant and to those who are nursing babies in those days. And pray that your flight may not be in winter or on the Sabbath. For then there will be great tribulation [= great travail] such as has not been since the beginning of the world until this time, no, nor ever shall be. And unless those days were shortened, no flesh would be saved; but for the elect's sake those days will be shortened (Matt 24:15-22, emphasis in NKJV).

There is no mistaking the focus in this passage on the nation of Israel. One can note the reference to the Jewish prophet Daniel, to "the holy place" (i.e., the Temple), to Judea, and to the Sabbath. Absolutely no instructions are given to Gentile believers even though the Great Travail is worldwide and threatens the extinction of humanity itself. The directions are for Israelis.

Nevertheless, His directions telling Israeli believers to flee are not contained in OT prophecy. Indeed, Matt 24:16-22 is basically all new.

Furthermore, the previous paragraph (24:9-14) has prepared us for this orientation to Israel. There Jesus had said (v 9), "you will be hated by *all nations*" [Gk., 'all the Gentiles']. He had also stated (v 14) that "this gospel of the kingdom will be preached in all the world as a witness to *all the nations* [Greek = 'all the Gentiles'], and then the end will come."

So Jesus speaks in Matt 24:9-21 as if, in this coming day, the evangelization of the Gentile world is once again in the hands of *Jews*.

These Israeli believers are aroused to flight by the appearance of the "abomination of desolation" in the Jewish Temple. Since the Temple was destroyed in AD 70, this also obviously implies the *rebuilding* of that Temple before this event can take place. This rebuilding is exactly what many Israelis today hope will happen.

The emphasis on Israel that I have noted is not surprising in the light of the whole discourse. As we have seen, when our Lord's coming (*parousia*) begins, He will "take along" with Him certain people (24:40-41). Even if we did not have the confirmation of the Apostle Paul in 1 Thessalonians, we could easily conclude that those whom Christ "takes along" at the beginning of His "coming" must be people who belong to Him.

In this way, as Paul puts it, Jesus "*delivers*" Christians "from the wrath to come" (1 Thess 1:10). They are *saved* from the world's "labor pains" in order to "live together with Him" (1 Thess 5:10).

This catching away of believers (that is, the Rapture) at the *start* of the *parousia* is described in more detail by Paul in 1 Thess 4:15-18. Paul certainly has this beginning point in mind as he makes clear by the words, "we who are alive and remain *until* the coming of the Lord" (Gk., *eis ten parousian*, "to [unto] the coming").

So when the *parousia* unexpectedly begins, every believer in the world will "be caught up...in the clouds to meet the Lord in the air" (1 Thess 4:17). Once that has happened, not a single believer will be left on earth.

However, during the "beginning of labor pains," while the Gentile nations are in turmoil (Matt 24:6-7), there will be people in Israel who believe in Jesus. The first converts could come from simply reading the NT Scriptures. By the time referred to in Matt 24:15, there will undoubtedly be many believers (see Rev 7:1-8; 14:1-5). They will be ready to obey the Lord's instructions given in 24:15-21.

We can see what is clearly implied in all this. Once all Christians on earth are caught up (raptured) by Jesus, God will start all over again with Israel.

In fact, God's Prophet envisions a situation in the land of Israel in which Jewish worship has been renewed in the Jewish Temple (Matt 24:15). His followers, therefore, ought to be prayerfully concerned that their flight not occur on the Sabbath day (24:20). The Jewish law severely restricts movements on that day. Implied in this, as well, is the fact that Jesus' disciples in Israel will be *observant* of the

Mosaic Law. This contrasts with believers today who are free from the law (see Gal 2:19-20).

All of this is eye opening.

The People Who Are Delivered by the Second Advent

Matthew 24:4-22 (as well as 24:23-35) is addressed to people who will live on earth *after* the Second Advent has started. But, as we have seen, Matt 24:36-41 reveals that there are people who will be *taken off the earth* as soon as the Second Advent begins. It is not their destiny to experience any part of the "wrath to come" during the world's labor pains.

Clearly these are people whose role in the purposes of God are not at all the same as those who will live during the Great Tribulation. God graciously rescues them when His Son descends from heaven as the Day of the Lord begins.

This rescue is not based on their own merits. On the contrary, God did not "appoint [them] to wrath, but to obtain salvation [deliverance] through our Lord Jesus Christ who died for [them]." As a result, they can "live together with Him" (1 Thess 5:9-10). This deliverance, therefore, is a gift of God's grace based on the death of Christ.

This is the point at which we need to call to mind an earlier prophecy spoken by Jesus Christ, God's Prophet. This too is recorded in the Gospel of Matthew, a book that has providentially become the first book in our NT.

The prophecy is found in Matt 16:17-18:

> Jesus answered and said to him, "Blessed are you, Simon Bar-Jonah, for flesh and blood has not revealed this to you, but My Father who is in heaven. And I also say to you that you are Peter, and on this rock *I will build My church*, and the gates of Hades shall not prevail against it" (emphasis added).

Jesus does not say here that "I *am* or *have been building* My church," but "I *will build* My church" This is plainly a prophecy. And as the Christian readers of Matthew would know (as we also do from the Book of Acts), the coming of the Holy Spirit on the day of Pentecost created the spiritual body that we call the Christian Church (note Acts 2:47; 5:11).

The Church is not, as many have wrongly thought, simply a collective term for all regenerate Jews and Gentiles throughout the ages. On the contrary, the Holy Spirit's coming accomplished something brand new.

By His baptizing work from Pentecost on, the Holy Spirit unites believers to the Body of Christ. This union transcends racial, social, and sexual identities so that men and women of all backgrounds are *one* in that body (1 Cor 12:12-13; Gal 3:27-29). As is made clear in John 7:37-39 (where Jesus prophesied the gift of the Spirit), He was speaking of the Spirit coming *after* His own return to heaven.

Correctly, then, Paul speaks of the Christian Church as a spiritual organism unrevealed to OT prophets (Eph 3:4-10). He describes it as "one new man" (Eph 2:14-15). The Church is also called "the household of God." It is growing "into a holy temple in the Lord" and serves as "a dwelling place of God *in the Spirit*" (Eph 2:19-22, emphasis added).

The so-called Second Temple of Judaism, that existed while Jesus was on earth, was doomed to destruction (Matt 24:1-2). In its place would rise, by the work of the Holy Spirit, a new, spiritual temple composed not of physical materials, but of believing people (see 1 Pet 2:1-5). As Jesus said (Matt 16:18), He Himself would be the Builder of this new Temple of God.

Therefore, the removal of the Church from the earth at the beginning of our Lord's *parousia* is the removal of this *spiritual* Temple from the earth. The rebuilt *physical* Temple referred to in Matt 24:15 is duly acknowledged by Jesus when He refers to it as "the *holy* place." The validity of the Sabbath law is also implied in v 20. The Church does not share this relationship to the Jewish system of worship, as the Book of Hebrews makes absolutely clear.

To put it simply, God will return to Israel as the focus of His program on earth. The recognition of this fact is the recognition of a fundamental NT truth by which the Church is clearly distinguished from regenerate national Israel.

Nevertheless, the Christian Church and regenerate national Israel are often thought to have exactly the same relationship to God. But this is a major error that theologians and pastors often make. The teaching of Jesus never reduces that nation's special status so that it is indistinguishable from the Church. Israel remains a distinct nation whose destiny is not submerged into the destiny of the Church.

On the contrary, Matt 24:4-22 makes clear that Israel, not the Church, will be at the center of God's concerns during the Great Travail.

So once the Second Advent begins, the Christian Church is completely absent from earth. The King of Israel is about to conquer the world.

The Two Relationships

Very simply put, national Israel and the Christian Church sustain different relationships to our Lord and Savior Jesus Christ. National Israel is His chosen race, the particular nation whose throne He will someday claim and from which He will rule the Gentiles as well (Luke 1:32-33; Rev 12:5). The Church is His Bride (Eph 5:31-32), and therefore His Queen (Ps 45:10-17).

This distinction has seemed to many to be an inappropriate dividing of the family of God, but human life has many built-in relational distinctions. Obviously a man's father and mother are distinct from his children, and a man's wife is quite distinct from both parents *and* children. All these people belong to the same extended family, but each sustains a special relationship to the man in question.

The effort often made to erase the distinction between national Israel and the Christian Church is similar to saying that there is no relational difference between a man's sister and his wife. It doesn't really make sense. It is also unbiblical.

What has emerged from our study thus far is an important fact. Our Lord's prophetic teaching carries with it the clear implication of different relationships. One group of people will be "taken along" with Him at the beginning of His coming (*parousia*). They will escape this whole period of divine judgment on the earth.

However, others, who subsequently believe in Jesus for eternal life, will *live through* that same period. This difference is easily understood if we know that those who are "taken along"—delivered—are part of the King's Bride, the Church. But the people described in Matt 24:15-22 are born again Israelis living under the law of Moses.

It is these people who will see the fulfillment of God's promises to the Jewish *nation*. That *nation* reemerged as one of the nations of the world in 1948, after many centuries as a people without a homeland. Our own country was the first to formally recognize the new state of Israel.

It takes a special form of blindness not to see that God is getting ready to fulfill the words of His greatest Prophet, Jesus Christ. Jesus clearly thought of the Church and national Israel as possessing quite distinct relationships to Himself.

Strikingly, this aspect of Jesus' thinking is reinforced in the two parables we have looked at previously. These were:

(1) The parable of the unprepared servant (Matt 24:45-51), and

(2) The parable of the unprepared women (Matt 25:1-13).

Both parables teach lessons that we need here and now. We should stay alert and ready for our Lord's return. We should not allow misconduct or neglect to leave us unprepared to meet Him. Yet despite these obvious lessons, these parables also reflect the differing situations of the Church and Israel.

In the parable of the unfaithful servant (Matt 24:45-51), the fundamental error of that servant is a simple one. In his heart he says, "My master is delaying His coming" (24:48). From this error of *heart* flow all his errors of *conduct*. This servant is still engaged in serious misconduct right up to the unexpected coming of his master.

Clearly this man represents those who will be living when the "coming of the Son of Man" occurs suddenly and without warning. Nothing interrupts this servant's misbehavior except his master's return. In other words, he does not pass through the earthshaking events of the Great Travail. In short, this servant is a representative of the Christian Church.

But things are different for the ten virgins of the second parable (Matt 25:1-12). The very thing that the servant in the first parable wrongly thinks about his master's coming is an actual reality for these women.

This fact is made extremely clear in the original Greek. In the first parable the servant thinks, "My master is delaying [Gk., *chronizei*] his coming" (24:48). But in the second parable we are told by Jesus Himself, "But while the bridegroom *delayed* [author's translation; Gk., *chronizontos*] they all slumbered and slept" (25:5).

Since the English of these two verses (in the NKJV) partially conceals this contrast, it may help to set out that contrast in English like this:

"'My master *delays* his coming'" (Matt 24:48, emphasis added).

"While the bridegroom *delayed*" (Matt 25:5, emphasis added).

What the servant *wrongly* thinks his master is doing in parable one, the bridegroom *actually does* in parable two. In parable two, he *does* delay. Furthermore, the wise virgins as well as the foolish ones take advantage of this delay to catch up on their sleep. They only wake up when the "midnight" cry is heard: "Behold, the bridegroom is coming." In the circumstances described in this parable, *sleeping is sensible!* For the servant in parable one, it would not have been sensible at all.

This fits the earliest section of the Olivet Discourse perfectly. Jesus gives His very *first* admonition in the discourse in Matt 24:6. His disciples are to see to it that they "are not troubled." This untroubled attitude is symbolized in parable two by *all* the virgins (including the wise ones) sleeping.

But then comes the "midnight" cry. This corresponds in parable two to Jesus' *second* admonition, given in Matt 24:15-18. The "abomination of desolation" must arouse His disciples to flee. This need to flee is symbolized in parable two by the words "go out to meet Him" (25:6; see 25:1). So when Jesus' faithful followers flee from Judea, in a spiritual sense they will be *going forth* to meet the Bridegroom.

But the Great Travail will be hard indeed. His disciples will be persecuted (Matt 24:9) and even betrayed (24:10). The times will be extremely trying. As stated in 24:12, "the love of many [believers] will grow cold [like a dying torch! (25:8)]."

Therefore during the Great Travail the disciples of Jesus will need *all of their spiritual resources.* They must be prepared to use these resources. In parable two, the wise virgins *are* prepared but the foolish ones *are not.*

One might think here of the need for diligent and prayerful attention to God's word during "the beginning of labor pains." In this way the disciples of Jesus in those days can procure true spiritual energy (the oil). That energy will be urgently needed to keep their testimony to Christ (their torches) burning brightly during the Great Travail.

There *will be* a testimony to Christ during the Great Travail (24:14), but this period will be the darkest night in all of human history. Those who keep their torches burning for Jesus Christ during such a period will have an honored role when the Bridegroom arrives on earth. But the ten virgins are *not* the Bride.

Therefore, when the two parables are closely considered, they reflect the differing positions of two bodies of believers. One of these is the Christian Church; the other is the believing portion of national Israel.

Parable one reflects the situation of the Church as the Lord begins His coming [*parousia*] suddenly and without warning. Parable two reflects the situation of believing Israel once the period of the world's birth pangs has begun to run its course. These disciples, especially, will understand that the labor pains are a prelude to the "birth" of a new age. They herald the establishment of the kingdom of God on earth.

There are two further points that support the observations just made. First, there is a "then" introducing parable two in Matt 25:1 (Greek = "then," "at that time" "thereupon." See BDAG, p. 1012). But to what does the expression "at that time" refer? Most naturally it refers back to the conclusion of the immediately preceding parable in Matt 24:45-51. The master of the slothful servant comes and deals with him (24:50-51). It is then that the situation of the *second* parable exists.

This agrees completely with our Lord's teaching in the Olivet Discourse as we have already seen it. The "coming of the Son of Man" (the *parousia*) introduces a new state of affairs, like the flood did in Noah's time. So the parable of the ten virgins awaits its fulfillment *after* Christ comes for the Church. It will take place *during* the Great Travail.

The second point is this. When the midnight cry is raised in parable two, the announcement is, "Behold, the bridegroom *is coming*" (25:6, emphasis added; the Greek verb here, in this context, expresses action in progress). In the setting of parable two, this statement clearly means that the bridegroom is now on his way and *getting close* to the banquet hall where the wedding celebration will take place.

So the time has arrived for the virgins to go out and meet him as he approaches. They will welcome him and go with him into the banquet hall.

For the ten virgins the bridegroom does *not* arrive without warning. Instead, there is a signal given when he is getting close. So, too, during the period of the world's "labor pains," there is a signal that time is running out. That signal is "the abomination of desolation...standing in the holy place." This desecration of God's Temple will be followed at once by the Great Travail. After that, "the Son of Man" will immediately appear (Matt 24:29-30).

The two parables in Matt 24:45–25:13 are a marvelous example of the teaching skill of God's Prophet, Jesus Christ. On one level both parables can be read as relevant to believers awaiting the beginning of our Lord's coming. Jesus applies them that way in 25:13.

But at a deeper level, the parables reveal subtle differences. At this deeper level, they distinguish between two groups of people: (1) those for whom His coming is *without warning* and (2) those who will be *looking for the warning* of the abomination of desolation. In short, the parables distinguish between the experience of the Church and the experience of Jewish believers after the Church is gone.

Needless to say, Jesus did not necessarily expect all these details to be obvious when the disciples first heard the parables. The general truth was obvious. They should not allow misconduct or spiritual neglect to leave them unprepared for His coming. But our Lord also knew that the parables would become part of Matthew's inspired Gospel. When that happened, they could be prayerfully studied and more deeply understood.

The words of our Lord Jesus Christ always reward deeper study. Like all inspired truth, His words always have unanticipated depth. That is emphatically true here.

The Manifestation of His Presence

As we have now seen, "the coming of the Son of Man" covers an extended period. His coming begins with the Rapture just as God's judgments start to fall on a world unprepared for them. The process of that coming continues through the period of "travail" on earth.

When the abomination of desolation stands in the rebuilt Jewish Temple, Jesus' Israeli disciples will know (like the ten virgins) that the Bridegroom is *on His way and getting close!*

Therefore, the Lord's descent into the clouds to rapture the Christian Church (see 1 Thess 4:16-17) is only the *first phase* of His return from heaven to earth. From a human perspective, after catching up the Church (His bride!) to Himself, He *slows down.* But no doubt this is *only* from a human perspective.

It would be foolish to try to literally measure "speed" in these circumstances. I admit I know no more than the Scriptures tell us.

However, according to the modern scientific concept of relativity (both special and general), the speed with which time passes is actually relative to the speed of the observer. If someone or something moves at the speed of light, no time passes at all. It is likely that from our Lord's perspective, and from ours once we are transformed, events on earth will move with enormous rapidity. Our time with Him in the clouds will probably seem very short indeed.

Nevertheless, it is *in the clouds* that He is revealed to all men on earth at the end of the Great Travail. As Jesus said, "immediately after the tribulation of those days" there will be heavenly phenomena (Matt 24:29). And it is *"then"* that "the sign of the Son of Man will appear in heaven." It is *"then"* that "all the tribes of the earth will mourn" and "see the Son of Man coming *on the clouds of heaven* with power and great glory" (24:30, emphasis added).

In other words, mankind sees Him *already* on the clouds where His Church has *already* met Him. The "coming" which began quite some time before (humanly speaking) is now manifest to all humanity.

Jesus' words clearly suggest that "the coming of the Son of Man" will have a "manifestation" at the conclusion of the Great Travail. Jesus' statements in 24:23-28 underline this conclusion. In those verses, our Lord teaches that during the Great Travail He will not be *secretly* revealed to men (24:23-26). Instead, He will be made known *openly* just like lightning flashes across the entire sky (24:27).

Following Matt 24:23-28, Jesus proceeds to describe this manifestation in 24:29-30. Paul also evidently understood Jesus' words in this way. He writes:

> And then the lawless one will be revealed, whom the Lord
> will consume with the breath of His mouth and destroy

with *the brightness of His coming* (2 Thess 2:8, emphasis added).

The Greek words translated by "the brightness of His coming" can be rendered "the *appearance* of His coming." Of special interest here is a technical use of the Greek noun for "appearance" (*epiphaneia*). This use is given in the latest edition of the standard NT Greek-English dictionary in this way:

> As a technical term relating to transcendence it refers to a visible and frequently sudden manifestation of a hidden divinity, either in the form of a personal appearance, or by some deed of power or oracular communication by which its presence is made known (BDAG, p. 385).

In addition to this, the word *parousia* ("coming") also has technical senses that are equally appropriate here. Quoting BDAG again (pp. 780-81):

> The use of *parousia* as a technical term has developed in two directions. On the one hand the word served as a sacred expression for the coming of a *hidden divinity*, who makes his presence felt by a revelation of his power, or whose presence is celebrated in the cult… On the other hand, *parousia* became the official term for a visit of a person of high rank, esp. of kings and emperors visiting a province (emphasis added).

So Paul's words ("the brightness of His coming") can refer to the sudden *manifestation* of the previously *concealed* arrival of the King of kings! In other words, His hidden arrival is suddenly revealed to the doom of "the lawless one" (that is, the first "Beast" of Revelation 13). The "coming of the Son of Man," that began when earthly life was proceeding as normal, is abruptly manifested.

We could therefore translate the words of 2 Thess 2:8 as follows:

> And then the lawless one will be revealed, whom the Lord will consume with the breath of His mouth and destroy with *the manifestation of His presence* (emphasis added).

This perspective is underscored also by Paul's words in 2 Thess 1:7-8 where he writes:

...when the Lord Jesus *is revealed from heaven* with His mighty angels, in flaming fire taking vengeance on those who do not know God (emphasis added).

The sudden appearance of the Son of Man in the clouds of heaven is nothing less than a "revelation from heaven" of His hidden "coming" or "presence" (*parousia*). The *manifestation of His coming* "on the clouds of heaven" will be visible to everyone on earth (Matt 24:30).

When this glorious revelation of His coming takes place, the Church will already be with her Bridegroom in the clouds (1 Thess 4:17). But His believing people, who were saved during the birth pangs of the new age, will be here on earth to see Him coming on those very clouds (Matt 24:30). They will welcome Him back to earth as their King.

The Olivet Discourse is a rich and effective exposition of prophecy. It is fundamental and indispensable to NT prophetic discussions. All the other NT writers who speak at any length of the end times (Paul, Peter and John) are indebted to this discourse. They owe their fundamental understanding of prophecy to the words of Jesus Christ, the greatest of all the prophets of God.

The Olivet Discourse is profitable for God's people in this age, before His coming begins, and for His Jewish people during earth's time of great distress after His coming is underway. Both groups can learn vital lessons from this discourse in their own different situations.

Gentile believers during the Great Travail can also learn much from this discourse. They can learn the truth about the days in which they will be living. In fact, the final section of the Olivet Discourse (25:31-46) is designed especially for Gentiles!

CHAPTER 18

Jesus' Words in the Contemporary Context

I n our own day and time the Olivet Discourse has been increasingly relegated to the margins of Christian consciousness. Many Christians who have read it have never studied it carefully. The result is that we are in danger of being suddenly overtaken by the very events Jesus has described.

This is the coming surprise that will catch our world off-guard. If it catches us by surprise, we will have only ourselves to blame.

Looking at the world we live in right now, it is hard to miss how preoccupied it is with the problem of Israel. Of course, we Americans are worried about the hostility of the Muslim world and the resulting terrorism. But at the same time, we know that much of this hostility arises from our support of the Jewish nation.

The Arab world would dearly love to expunge the state of Israel from the Middle East. The president of Iran has called for exactly that. But the Muslim states know this will be impossible as long as the United States continues to support that nation.

We may already be moving toward a treaty arrangement of the type prophesied in Dan 9:27. The terrorist group Hamas, which now controls the Palestinian parliament, has been reported to be open to a truce with Israel for a specified period of time. Perhaps the seven-year covenant of Dan 9:27 will be called a "truce."

This is hardly the time to be forgetting about prophetic truth, even though many evangelical Christians are doing just that. It is hardly the time either to be making a theological case for the error of the unfaithful servant who said, "My master is delaying his coming" (Matt 24:48).

In effect, that is precisely what some theologians are doing when they argue that Jesus cannot come immediately because the Great Tribulation must come first. Such doctrine is not only wrong, it is spiritually dangerous.

As we have seen, the judgments begin when His coming begins. The doctrine that they must *precede* it is a grave error. Such a doctrine encourages us *not to expect* that our Lord might come at any time. It makes people think that He will "delay" His coming until *after* the events of the Tribulation.

Simply put, it is an unwitting theological articulation of the *error* of the unfaithful servant.

Now is the time to listen carefully to the words of Jesus, God's Prophet. Our Lord *will* take the Christian Church "along with" Him some day. And He *will* then turn His attention fully to Israel and to its role in this world. It doesn't really matter how many people don't think so. Reality is not determined by popular opinion. It is determined by the purposes of God.

Our Savior's words *will be fulfilled*! Perhaps that will happen very soon indeed.

At the very beginning of these future events, our Lord will catch up to Himself every person on earth who belongs to Him. That is, He will take with Him everyone who has believed in Him for the free gift of everlasting life (see John 3:16; 5:24; 6:47). In the twinkling of an eye, we will be in His glorious presence.

As Paul said, Jesus "died for us, that…we should live together with Him" (1 Thess 5:10). It is only the sacrificial death of Christ, in payment for our sins, that makes this possible. It is the death of Christ that allows a holy God to give eternal life to sinners like us. We receive that gift when we believe in His Son for it.

Unless we have that life, we cannot live together with Him when He comes. If we do not have that kind of life, He will not take us along with Him at His coming.

Will He take you with Him when He comes?

If not, or if you are not sure, you can be sure right now. Jesus said, "*Most assuredly, I say to you, he who believes in Me has everlasting life*" (John 6:47, emphasis added). Believe these words and you *are* ready to live with Him forever.

And if you *have* believed, then stay awake and be fully alert. Don't allow sinful conduct or spiritual neglect to rob you of your readiness to meet Him face to face. You have a splendid promotion ahead of you if you are faithful. Jesus said,

> And he who overcomes, and keeps My works until the end, to him I will give power over the nations—"He shall rule them with a rod of iron..." as I also have received from My Father (Rev 2:26-27).

And since Revelation was written to Christian churches (Rev 22:16), near its climax Jesus gives them a powerful exhortation. As the Apostle John is about to describe the "end of the age," his words are suddenly *interrupted*. God's greatest Prophet, Jesus, then gives one last warning to the churches about *the coming surprise*.

Rooted in the Olivet Discourse, His words are these:

> Behold, I am coming as a thief. Blessed is he who watches [*grēgorōn*], and keeps his garments, lest he walk naked and they see his shame (Rev 16:15).

The unfaithful servant of Matthew 24 was stripped of his role as a servant, and experienced shame for his hypocrisy (24:51). But the servant who serves well, because he is watching, will be truly "blessed"—both here and hereafter.

Scripture Index

Subject Index

CPSIA information can be obtained at www.ICGtesting.com
Printed in the USA
LVOW04s0218191114

414339LV00036B/2482/P